Spiritual And Political Revolutions In Islam

SPIRITUAL AND POLITICAL
REVOLUTIONS IN ISLAM

BY

FELIX VALYI

LONDON:
KEGAN PAUL, TRENCH, TRUBNER & CO., LTD.
BROADWAY HOUSE: 68-74, CARTER LANE, E.C.
1925

Printed in Great Britain by MACKAYS LTD., Chatham.

PREFACE

THE title of this book may at first sight appear somewhat pretentious. The whole of the Musulman world is in a state of fermentation, whilst in the following pages the author has only treated one or two aspects of the racial conflicts that have bathed the Near East in rivers of blood and have had such disastrous effects upon the fate of Europe. Nevertheless, the transformation of the Musulman nations which is taking place under our eyes with a rapidity which has surprised even the wisest observers, can only be designated by the word *Revolution* in its widest significance—that is to say, a revolution at once political and spiritual. It is a tremendous upheaval of which we can here only describe a few aspects, and we beg the indulgence of the reader for any discrepancies there may be in a book which was written from time to time as the various problems with which it deals were presented to the author.

The essay on the origins of the Armenian Problem deals only with the period ending with the Russian Revolution of 1917—a period the documentation for which seemed to the author sufficient for placing the responsibility for the massacres in Asia Minor partly on the shoulders of the Tsarist Government. As for the events subsequent to 1917, and particularly for the part played by the Western Powers in the development of the Armenian problem down to the time of the Conference of Lausanne (1923) the author was of opinion that the historical documentation accessible was insufficient for the purposes of an impartial enquiry. Nevertheless the most superficial observer cannot help seeing that Russian methods in the East have undergone no change, and that behind the façade of the Bolshevik Revolution the same expansion on the part of Russia is still menacing the interests of all the free nations. It would, therefore, be a most unpardonable error on the part of Musulmans to allow themselves to be hypnotized by the pompous phrases issuing from Moscow.

If the following pages succeed in shedding a little light on the great problem of the relations between East and West, they will have accomplished their object.

October, 1924.

CONTENTS

INTRODUCTION

Europe and Asia

At this moment, when the material passions consuming the soul of Europe are manifested in a form of diplomacy entirely devoid of science and ideas, and threaten once again to shatter the peace of the whole world, it behoves us to study, with care and precision, those lessons of history and those fundamental truths upon which the future depends.

The crisis reached by the spirit of the West in its dealings with the nations of Asia and Africa is apparent to all. The white race is undergoing one of those attacks of conscience, which, at certain moments in history, upset the established order of things, shake Governments and Empires to their foundations, and provoke all kinds of antagonistic forces which in a latent state, from times immemorial, are to be seen accompanying the evolution of mankind, doomed to suffering.

History, confronted by these prodigious phenomena of universal dissolution and social and economic disintegration, stands perplexed. It has not yet succeeded in understanding the mystery of the human soul, which, under periodical assaults of collective frenzy, frivolously pulls to pieces what it has taken centuries of painful effort and struggle to accomplish.

The extraordinary state of affairs that we are witnessing to-day arises from the doubt which is beginning to take hold of the finest minds in the Western world, concerning the justice of the Western attitude towards those peoples whom we have acquired the vicious habit of regarding as no more than human cattle fit to be sacrificed on the altar of modern industrialism. With the object of ensuring the greater comfort of the white race, two-thirds of humanity have been reduced to economic slavery. The very same Bible, in the name of which all men were declared equal, and with the help of which the first Christians destroyed the idol of ancient civilization—the Roman Empire—this same Gospel is now being used to-day in order to justify before the whole of the Christian world the subjection of non-Christian humanity.

It is now over fifty years ago since the Science of Religion, after having abandoned the narrow outlook of theological sectarianism, and having applied itself with zeal to the study of the original documents at the root of mankind's great religions, succeeded in convincing us that both Buddha and Mohammed are the worthy coadjutors of Jesus in the task of establishing the Kingdom of God on earth. The accidental differences which history has found between the cities raised by men ought not to blind an impartial mind to the fact that the City of God was the ultimate ideal of all the great founders of spiritual edifices intended for the refuge of those souls that feel abashed before the profound mystery of the Universe. The Science of Religion, in the name of which the cultured world has just celebrated Renan's hundredth anniversary, has long since gazed beyond the horizon of missionaries and theologians of the old school. It admires the work of Buddha and Mohammed on the same principle that it admires that of Jesus; and pays homage to the moral beauty of Islam and the higher philosophy to be found in the purest of India's sacred books with the same feelings of gratitude with which it reads the Sermon on the Mount.

In spite of this scientific truth, universally recognized by the whole of the intellectual *élite* of the world, in spite of the noble efforts now being made towards a universal brotherhood and the moral unity of all civilizations, a certain number of utterly obnoxious tendencies still continues to hold the ignorant masses of both the West and the East as far as possible asunder. These tendencies, which aim exclusively at material profit, control by means of the vilest passions not only the bulk of the modern Press, but also the bureaucracy and diplomacy of the day, and even succeed in contaminating science, philosophy, and the impartial investigations of historians. The outcome of this attitude of mind reveals itself in all its hideousness in every discussion concerning the East, both in Europe and America.

Instead of acknowledging the moral and spiritual nature of a problem which has been mishandled for centuries, the political and religious leaders of the West persist in the error of confounding the soul of minor sects with the dividends which must be guaranteed to their "protectors," who are rarely disinterested. We find merchants, incapable of thought, protesting against a policy of justice towards Asia, in order that they may not forfeit, even for a short space, material advantages often acquired by unjust means. The petition presented by the manufacturers of Lancashire, two years ago, to the Secretary of State for India, with the view of abolishing the protective measures taken by the Legislative Assembly of India in favour of the Indian native industries which are trying to free themselves from the clutches of foreign commercial greed, proceeds from the same bigoted standpoint which to-day urges the silk manufacturers of Lyons and the Chambers of Commerce at Constantinople to protest against the economic independence of Turkey.

In all these cases the object is to prevent non-European nations from developing in a manner compatible with their own interests, in order that certain small commercial groups in Europe may realize immoderate gains. A problem of great moral significance is thus converted before the eyes of ill-informed Europe into a concern about profit and loss.

The question of the East has entered upon a phase which constrains us to regard from a different standpoint all those matters upon which the future relations of Europe and Asia depend. Henceforward the civilized peoples of Asia must no longer be flung as natural prey to a hotchpotch of Levantines and industrial adventurers ; we must grant to Asia the legitimate rights of Man, the Law of Nations, on a basis of equality of treatment. This is what the Continent of Asia is asking for, through the voice of its chosen few ; and this accounts for the fact that the whole of Asia and Islam are united with Turkey and Angora in their struggle against the sordid covetousness of the West and against the policy of partition so eloquently exposed in the nineteenth century by the French historian, Albert Sorel.

The policy of plunder is at the root of all the recent calamities that have overtaken humanity. If it be admitted that in prehistoric times the primitive character of the races, let loose upon the fertile tracts of the earth, situated in the only temperate climes then known, accounts for the savage struggles that ensued for the possession of pasture-lands and dwelling-places, there is no longer any sound reason for refusing to divide the good things of the earth afresh, among all nations, on a basis of equality and justice. Political and economic equality must go hand in hand in international affairs, if the equilibrium of the Continents and States is to be restored.

The historical influences which are agitating humanity, by making their final consequences felt in the domain of world politics, prove to those who have eyes to see, how fatally a disturbed equilibrium recoils upon those who are responsible for all the upheavals and the chaos. The Russian, the German, and the Hapsburgian Empires were the victims of their own methods of partition both in Europe and in Asia. The interdependence of the two continents is one of those truths which is wilfully scouted by the historical and political sciences of Europe; nevertheless, the meanest historical vision might have foreseen that the question of the East will ultimately reverse all the terms of a problem, which, thanks to a false conception of the mission of the white race on earth, has been perverted for centuries.

The question to-day is, whether there still remains a sufficient number of intelligent Europeans capable of realizing that Asia is demanding insistently to be allowed, on equal terms, to join the movement of modern ideas, and that it behoves us to promote this reintegration of Asiatic people into the family of nations by co-operating with them intellectually, scientifically, and economically. By admitting Japan to the Law of Nations we have but taken the first step in a development which must inevitably lead, from the standpoint of the future, to a revision of all our views concerning the value of non-Christian civilizations.

Islam, which, for a very considerable period, has been the greatest force aiming at the organization of the people and communities spread over half of Asia, is now being stirred by certain changes of thought—all tending towards science and progress—the power of which is irresistible. When the Emir of Afghanistan received the first British Ambassador at Kabul, after the conclusion of the Anglo-Afghan Treaty of November, 1921, he intentionally laid stress upon the solidarity of the Mohammedan nations confronted by external greed ; but he also declared with great sincerity, how eager the peoples of Islam were to become acquainted with modern science, and how anxious his own people were, in view of the economic revival of Central Asia, to conclude an Anglo-Afghan alliance.

Mustafa Kemal Pasha adopted the same friendly tone towards the West, whose scientific co-operation he hoped to obtain in the task of raising up the people of Asia Minor.

In both of these cases, as in the case of China and India, we are not concerned with anti-European fanatics, or aggressive Pan-Islamism or Pan-Buddhism, but with a spiritual movement based upon a national sentiment bred under the influence of Western teaching—a sentiment which Islam and the other religions of Asia are turning to account as powerful moral forces, capable of effecting the fusion of the many different races whose solidarity and fraternal unity is the object desired.

The profound beauty of the movement, which produced Mustafa Kemal in the Musulman world and Gandhi in India, has not yet been understood by Europe. The conqueror of Angora, unlike the Indian sage, is far from being spurned by Europe, in spite of the fact that their aims are the same and that they differ only in the methods they adopt. Gandhi, albeit he is opposed in principle to violent methods, was cast into prison for certain articles he published in *Young India*, while Mustafa Kemal, owing to the fact that he had recourse to the very strategical and technical methods which Gandhi despises, is now dictating his will like a master. Nevertheless, their desires for national and human dignity appear to me identical. The one, relying on the military virtues of his race, demands the admission of Turkey into the family of independent States. The other, invoking the abstract ideal of Indian philosophy, the keynote of which is passivity, preaches a sort of passive and pacific nationalism. The one who fought Europe with European weapons was right in the eyes of Europe ; whilst he who loyally helped England during the war, and enabled her to mobilize Indian troops against the Turks in 1915, was sent to prison like a common felon. The system which, thanks to a strange irony of history, led to this result, proves that there is something rotten in the relations of Asia and Europe.

This rottenness in our ideas about Asia and Islam arises from the religious and social prejudices which poison the air between the two continents. And these prejudices are proof even against the overwhelming evidence of science and the ordinary conventions of international relations. When the Crown Prince of Japan visited the King of England two years ago, and was received with every mark of respect by the Royal Family and the Government, a number of English people, who were alleged to be ladies and gentlemen, preferred to leave a certain hotel in London, rather than take their seat at the same table with the captain and other officers of the Japanese man-of-war that had brought the hereditary prince of the most advanced and progressive Asiatic nation to England.

This refusal to shake hands with an Asiatic, or to take a meal with him, and this habit of regarding a man of the race of Buddha or Confucius, however cultivated he may be, as unworthy of a white man, although the latter may be a booby, has done more harm than all the economic methods by means of which Europe has placed its foot upon the neck of

Asiatic peoples. The moral problem which dominates the relations of England and Asia is at the root of the Eastern question.

All that is happening in India and in the countries of Islam only confirms this view. Every European who has had a correct grasp of the problem has been received with friendship by the East, and listened to with respect. The hatred which simmers among the masses of Asia has never prevented the *élite* among the Musulmans or Indians from listening attentively to moderate counsels, whenever these have come from true friends of Islam or of Asia. The first concern of the Egyptian Delegation which came to Europe in 1919 was to appeal to a celebrated English lawyer, in order to be advised concerning the Law of Nations. Angora is happy to welcome all foreigners who come imbued with a spirit of good will. Gandhi himself was educated at an English University, and he gave up a lucrative career as a lawyer, in order to devote himself to the service of his country. Mohammed Ali, who, with his brother, has also been sent to prison, paid his respects to the Pope when he was in Europe, and sought the friendship of European Universities, after having waited in vain for Oxford, where he had been educated, to hold out the hand of friendship to him.

It is difficult to maintain that all these Asiatics and Africans are simply criminals. It is very much more probable that Anglo-Indian bureaucracy knows nothing of the psychology of Islam or of Asia, and that the conclusion of the celebrated dialogue in Anatole France's *Etui de Nacre*, where the author depicts the Governor of Judea as hardly remembering the great revolutionary and innovator whom he allowed to be crucified, on information received from the Romans, might well be applied to Lord Reading. When the present Viceroy, who is a Jew, began his career in India, his speeches seemed to show his readiness to study and examine the standpoint of others with due respect. He even alluded to the terms of perfect equality on which his own race lived with the English people, in order to prove that the Anglo-Saxons can be just to other races, provided these are loyal to them. Very soon after his arrival in India he invited Mahatma Gandhi to Simla in the most friendly way, and the five or six interviews that took place between the Viceroy and the spiritual head of India were among the most impressive and affecting incidents to which the great Asiatic Drama has ever led.

Why was it necessary for Gandhi to go to prison, rather than to come to some understanding with that skilled designer of judicial compromises, that, throughout his career as a barrister and Chief Justice, Lord Reading has shown himself to be ? It was no accidental obstacle that wrecked the Viceroy's endeavours to placate the soul of India by gentle means.

Between the bureaucratic mentality in which the Viceroy, inexperienced in Indian affairs, soon became imprisoned, and the religious mentality of Gandhi there soon arose the great barrier erected by the average Englishman's pseudo-humanitarian education. The religious and racial prejudices, which are deeply rooted in the character of the average Englishman who prefers golf and cricket to the sport of ideas, prevented and will continue to prevent for some time to come well-meaning Englishmen who are beginning to come to the fore, from reforming the education of their country in so far as it affects the question of races.

The rooted incapacity of the average Englishman to understand the fundamental problem of the British Empire is indeed a strange tragedy.

An extraordinary accident—Providential or otherwise—has gathered together in one formidable organization four-fifths of the terraqueous globe under the ægis of an Imperial race. After two hundred years of growth, the Empire reached its apogee from the standpoint of territorial expansion. And at the very moment when humanity in a spirit of fraternity has begun to concentrate all its noblest aspirations upon a fusion of all civilizations, this Empire appears stubbornly to resist every new impulse of generosity and of understanding in regard to Asia, which is the one continent that has been the cradle of all human greatness, and all British greatness, and is likely to be the cradle of all greatness to come. The critical condition which has overtaken the British Empire, as well as the whole of Western civilization, is due to the faulty education both of the Englishman and average European. The ultimate cause of all the ills that threaten humanity is to be found in the Gladstonian attitude of mind, the ramifications of which extend throughout the whole of the Christian world from Canterbury to Athens.

With the object of upholding the validity of this analysis, by means of the inexorable methods used by a doctor, who must not conceal the truth from his patients, lest they should die of their ailments, we propose to place our finger on the moral disease that is raging in the heart of Europe. The Western world, that peninsula of the Continent of Asia, from it once upon a time derived all its religious and philosophical ideas, and from which it continues to draw all the raw materials necessary to its existence, despises both the spirit and the races of the Asiatic world. A small minority of enlightened Europeans apart, the bulk of the white race are full of preconceived ideas, superannuated prejudices, unfounded judgments, and historical absurdities concerning Asia and Islam, and concerning the part played by Asiatic civilizations in general. Even the Universities of the West are too prone to neglect the history of Asia. In the circumstances, therefore, how is it possible for the average European, who is called upon to do business in Asia, to be anything else than prejudiced, or to concern himself with loftier matters than the sordid question of profit and loss when, face to face with his Asiatic customers, he has occasion to judge Asiatic problems?

The problem is of a kind both moral and spiritual. That is why it is essential that the enlightened few of Europe and Asia, whose souls have remained uncorrupted, should unite together for the accomplishment of the mighty task of effecting an intellectual understanding between their two worlds.

The number of people whose goodwill can be relied upon is sufficiently great in all conscience, and if they could be united into one body, possessed of a deep knowledge of Western science, a friendly attitude towards the East, and a love of humanity freed from all racial or religious prejudices, they would, with the incommensurable weight of an entirely new spirit directed towards the good of Asia, and not towards the wretched material profits of Europe, compel the world to pay some heed to the spiritual and moral aspirations of these two-thirds of mankind, whom the mad stampede after lucre would fain condemn to perpetual economic slavery.

If the Western world, in the light of a new ideal, does not start a holy crusade against all war-profiteers, whether of the past or the future, the critical pass at which all Empires and States have arrived will not be survived, and we shall be compelled in the near future to be the helpless witnesses of sacrifices quite as bloody as those which have occurred in the past.

As Mr. Walter Elliot, M.P., in a fine passage that occurs in one of his articles published in the *Nineteenth Century*,* says:

"In 1918 the autumn of the victories left the West everywhere unchallengeable in arms and bankrupt in ideas." And his conclusion amounts to this, that, instead of combating with brutal force the powerful new movement of ideas, inspired by national policy, which is shaking the Continent of Asia, we should change our old ideas for new ones, and thus rejuvenate the moral relations of Europe and Asia by means of science and humanity.

Lord Ronaldshay, an ex-Governor of Bengal, in proposing a new economic programme for India, in the same publication, was not afraid to acknowledge the spiritual motives that actuate Gandhi and Das in opposing Western industrialism. But it should not be forgotten that Gandhi himself has made use of the railways built by the English, and that his successor, Das, still appears in an automobile surrounded by crowds of his followers.

The East has never refused to be taught at the Sorbonne, at the Collège de France, at the Ecole Polytechnique, and at Oxford and Cambridge.

* See the issue for January, 1923.

What she refuses to do, is to allow herself to be shamelessly exploited by Western profiteers, the deepest motive of whose souls is to prefer a pound sterling or a dollar to the most sublime idea capable of establishing peace on earth.

THE TURKISH REVOLUTION AND THE FUTURE OF ISLAM

I

"WHOEVER sees," said Mohammed, "sees to his own profit: whoever is blind is so at his own expense." The East is knocking impatiently at the door of Western Europe, and demands its seat at the Round Table of Nations. The Moslim East, in particular, asks in the name of an ancient and illustrious civilization to be allowed, for the sake of its own interests, to share in the schemes of international co-operation. Originally the creation of sincere thinkers, these schemes have been appropriated by hypocritical politicans for the benefit of their supporters, and are confused, vague, and cumbersome in practice when it is a matter of regulating the eternal struggle of the human passions. But the dramatic conflict between the East and the West, which from time immemorial has been presented on the screen of History, is assuming a new aspect and becoming more and more bitter from day to day. And in so far as Modern Democracy has shown itself incapable of dealing with the problem, the horizon of Humanity becomes ever more overcast. Wherefore it behoves us all the more to instil into our ideas that minimum of clarity without which we have no right to call ourselves "thinking beings."

Nietzsche has already pointed out the extent to which the destinies of European civilization are bound up with the Problem of Asia. In his *Beyond Good and Evil* he speaks with mingled fury and contempt of that Europe, which is but a wretched peninsula of the Continent of Asia, arrogating to herself spiritual superiority merely because she has invented modern mechanical devices, but has hitherto utterly failed to grasp the Spirit of Asia, the creator of all the great religions and philosophic ideas which constitute our moral being.

Recent events have fully justified Nietzsche's intuitive vision.

Economic science has indeed tried to reduce all social phenomena to a question of facts, figures, and formulæ. But the moral and spiritual side of human problems has just wreaked a formidable revenge upon the materialistic school of thought, on the economists of every category who have so long refused to give any consideration to Asia, because she possessed no industries, a fact which, in their eyes, meant that she was uncivilized. And now, awakened from her false belief in the science of international trade, the West finds itself faced by a new and disquieting form of the eternal Eastern question. The problem which was first raised by the material greed of Europe and was afterwards camouflaged into a religious question by the rhetoric of the Churches has, since the Great War, developed into a problem of moral and spiritual magnitude—that of balancing the historic forces which sway humanity.

Among these historic forces, Islam is one of the greatest spiritual and moral factors which we have to take into account if we wish to settle the problem of future relations between Europe and Asia. This is why the transformation of Turkey is of far graver importance than the mere number of inhabitants in Asia Minor would seem to imply. That is why, in its deeper significance, it goes beyond the bounds of European diplomacy, which has so long been the slave of obsolete formulæ, and, faithful to its accustomed traditions, can only point frantically to monetary advantages in Turkey, instead of trying to understand what no European statesman has ever succeeded in grasping. Just consider all the commercial, financial, and bureaucratic grievances that were brought at the Eastern Conference at Lausanne against the Turks as a Musulman nation; read the petitions of the French Chamber of Commerce in Constantinople in favour of economic privileges; follow the ecclesiastical discussion in the Anglo-Saxon world on the subject of the menace to Christian interests in the Near East, and the petitions signed by a whole host of Archbishops and leaders of various religious organizations in Europe and by the Federation of Churches in America. At the base of these impassioned appeals you will always find a false idea of Islam and of the Spirit of Asia. That is why I entreat you to-day to pay far more attention to the spiritual aspects of the Eastern situation, of Islam and Turkey especially, than to considering the dangers now threatening business profits in the East. To-day the hope of a spiritual unification of the world depends above all upon the transformations that may be looked for sooner or later in the soul of Asia, and particularly in the soul of Islam.

Islam, whose immense unexploited wealth raised so much international jealousy in the past, can only be understood and appeased if a sympathetic hearing is given to its voice, to its demand for equity. In order to exploit the treasure hidden in the soil of Musulman countries the friendship of Islam must first be won. And, in the long run, this friendship cannot be bought by petty diplomatic means, but demands, above all, an attitude of sympathy towards the soul of the East. The movement which has brought about so great a change in Asia Minor is not quite understood in the West. As it may well mark not only a turning-point in the history of Turkey, but exercise an influence far beyond her frontiers, I believe it to be worth my while to dwell briefly on its origin and its character, and to give you my reading of the political thought which underlies it. My object is solely to enlighten you as to actual facts and as to the soul of the New Turkey. I neither wish to take up any particular sectarian attitude nor to make the apologia of one man, however much I admire Mustafa Kemal.

II

The problem of the future relations of Western Europe with the Moslim world and with the continent of Asia in general remains the centre of world politics, and constitutes their most fateful and fundamental question. From the Bosphorus to the Ganges, from Baku to Herat, from Angora to Kaboul, to Delhi and Simla, Calcutta and Bombay, the same fundamental problem is everywhere found, the same question raised as to whether Europe and Asia, East and West, will come to an amicable understanding regarding the reconstruction of a habitable world, or whether, from lack of courageous guides and superior minds in Europe, the latter continent, besotted by a purely material civilization, will finally succumb in the merciless struggle with Asia.

The great economic plans that are being discussed in connection with the reconstruction of Europe can only be realized if the Eastern problem in all its ramifications is settled upon a fresh basis that shall be in keeping with the fundamental demands of common sense—the consent of the governed to a government by the constitutional methods best adapted to their needs, free from brutal violence or commercial selfishness, and strictly in accordance with the essential interests of the governed. The unscrupulous economic exploitation of one nation by another is no longer possible for any length of time. The same economic and psychological considerations that gave rise to the American War of Independence in 1776 are now convulsing the Continent of Asia, and the same political, or rather merely human wisdom which has succeeded in keeping Canada, Australia and South Africa within the framework of a great Commonwealth, might even now disarm the fierce hatred that is mustering its forces in the East. All the grandiose plans for world-wide reconstruction are doomed to failure unless the West is prepared to find a suitable place for the Eastern nations which are knocking impatiently at the gates of the Western world.

Among those nations Turkey has far greater importance than the actual geographical area of which she has been the incontestable ruler since the Treaty of Lausanne. Access to the most important highways leading from Europe to Asia is held by the Turkish race, and it is only with their permission, or across their political corpse, that the diplomat or the business-man, wishing to transact his affairs in the

Near and Middle East, is able to pass on his way. He who rules over Islam, whether by the sword or by the heart, be he Turk, English, French, or Russian, holds the keys of the Continent of Asia. He who allows these keys to slip from his fingers, no matter if he be lord over vast areas in Asia, can never feel that he is safe. The importance of the Turkish nation lies precisely in the fundamental fact, demonstrated by five centuries of diplomatic history, that upon her hinges the general relationship of the Great Powers to Asia. The intellectual and sentimental ties which bound Constantinople to Delhi in the very midst of an Anglo-Turkish war, prove the truth of this contention. The trifling but significant fact that even Lloyd George was obliged to invite leading Indian Musulmans to take part in this dramatic discussion between the British Empire and the Turks is a greater proof of the importance of Turkey to England than a hundred pages of historical argument. In fact, it may be boldly affirmed that in the present century, so pregnant with immense possibilities, the fate of the British Empire is intimately bound up with that of Islam.

This is why the attitude of Turkey towards Islam remains the key to the problem of Western and Central Asia: a great fighting nation, with great traditions, like Turkey, may determine the future development of all Moslim peoples, provided that her desire for Western culture be understood in this country. During the national struggle in Asia Minor, between 1919 and 1923, the fundamental question was whether the Turkish nation was to be made the advanced guard of Islamic Revolution against Europe, or whether she was to be allotted the rôle she aspired to play in the happiest moments of her dramatic historical career—that of the rear-guard to the West on the confines of the two continents of Europe and Asia. Were the Turks to be for or against Europe? This was not a matter of indifference in the midst of present-day chaos, when little nations who are less proud and less conscious of their past greatness, have been able to make themselves, according to circumstances, useful or dangerous to the cause of Western civilization. In fact, the power of Turkey is one of the most active and restless forces in Asiatic politics. Surely it is not quite impossible to deal with the Turk in a spirit of friendliness, with some readiness to understand him, and some ability in turning psychological factors to account, especially since he has decided to apply himself to the internal development of Asia Minor, and since he demands but one thing, and that is his right to live and to remain a nation among the nations.

Ever since the Turk made his first appearance in history, Europe has tried to find a means of turning him out of it, and of putting an end to the important part he has been playing in it for the last six hundred years. After two hundred years of agony the "three continents and three seas," dominion over which was so proudly specified among the titles of the Khalif of Stamboul, are to-day no more than an historical memory. Under the hammer-strokes of fate, the Turkish nation simplified her fundamental problem from the geographical and political standpoint by becoming what she had been when, in the middle of the thirteenth century, she knocked at the door of the Seldjukide Empire—a nation that looked for a livelihood. On her national soil, which Nature herself seems to have intended for her use, seeing that she has made her the predominating people in Asia Minor, the Turkish nation, every time that her position seemed to be threatened by the many rivals who have covetously watched her for centuries, has only regained fresh vigour. When the Russian Revolution demolished the political schemes that Tsarism had been elaborating ever since Peter the Great, the Turk came forth upon the diplomatic stage like a power rejuvenated.

How was it that the extraordinary change wrought by the Russian Revolution in the factors constituting the complex of the Eastern problem did not redound to the benefit of the Western Powers who, in 1918, seemed destined to recover the political direction of the movement of reform in the East? How was it that Islam, which during the nineteenth century had learned to look towards London and Paris, began to turn its attention to .Moscow, where a doctrine fundamentally opposed to Mohammedanism governs a race which, until the year 1917, the East regarded as its hereditary foe? This stupendous change in the scenery and the cast of the Oriental drama is simply due to the stupidity of public opinion in Europe, which, owing to its artificial subjection to the least disinterested and most prejudiced of Levantine influences, has never understood that the fate of Western civilization itself depends upon the great game now being played out between Moscow and Asia. English public opinion is far from understanding the importance of the fact that the great highways uniting our Continent with the most distant corners of Asia are in the hands of Islam, they traverse the very body of Turkey and of other Moslim nations, and they can serve the useful purpose of arteries in the world's economic life only on condition that the bodies through which they run possess the necessary modicum of vitality. Eternal geographical laws have, from time immemorial, made these international highways the real objectives of all great historical conflicts. As long as the Turkish nation holds the keys of the more important of these highways, the Western Powers have to reckon with her, uninfluenced by any anti-Turkish theories.

Unfortunately, a kind of phraseology dear to theological thinkers has obscured the question, which would certainly not have brought so much misery upon the human race if a spurious humanitarianism had not taken possession of it, and if it had remained what it was when diplomacy was conscious of its will—that is to say, a problem of the balance of world power. Truth to tell, European politicians have never been able to shake themselves free from theological bias, particularly in regard to Islam, and Christianity has always continued to prosecute the religious policy of preceding centuries, a policy infected with the prejudices which Byzantine chroniclers bequeathed to Western thought. These chroniclers were the great initiators of the anti-Moslim movement, and perverted European judgment regarding Oriental matters by such trumpery assertions as defeated nations usually make in order to wreak their vengeance upon their conquerors, and to comfort themselves in their humiliation. For a long while Byzantine sources of information constituted the basis of all European prejudices regarding the Near East, and the politicians of the Christian Powers readily turned them to account, as long as Christianity was exposed to the Turkish danger. One of the Popes, Pius II., the great humanist, known by the name of Æneas Sylvius, before organizing his crusade against the Turks, thought of an exceedingly simple way of solving the Ottoman problem. In a personal letter he invited Mohammed the Conqueror to become converted to Christianity, together with all his people, and promised to reward him by hailing him as the Supreme Head of Christianity and the protector of European order. This letter is but the symbol of the real charge that Europe brings against Turkey. Europe would have been prepared to forgive her all her conquests, which were no worse than those of any other conqueror. if only she had chosen to enter the Christian family, as all those other new nations had done who had migrated into Europe after the triumph of the Christian faith.

Even at the present day, European politicians still labour under this theological bias in regard to the peoples of Islam, a fact which has enabled all contending parties in the Near Eastern question to flaunt the most beautiful humanitarian theories, and to speculate upon the sentiments of solidarity which unite Europe with the so-called Christians of the East. Nothing was better calculated to impair the relations of Modern Europe with Islam. Nothing was more likely to obscure the real issue of the Asiatic problem. And nothing was more certain to threaten the peace of the world. Just as the theological standpoint applied to inter-European questions was the origin of all the troubles which disturbed our Continent during the religious wars, and just as Europe was able to breathe freely only when her destiny was taken out of the hands of the fanatics of religious politics, so a doctrinaire humanitarianism allied with Russian orthodox and Anglican political theology could only end catastrophically in the Near East, where it provoked all the worst passions to excess.

In English political literature two schools of ideas existed with regard to Turkey and Islam. In 1856 was published, in Edinburgh, Richard Cobden's famous pamphlet, *Russia, by a Manchester Manufacturer*, in which the head of the Manchester School combated the growing anti-Russian sentiments of English public opinion, and openly joined those who, in the name of Christianity, recommended the dismemberment of Turkey in favour of Russia, and declared that England had everything to gain economically by this alteration of the map of the Near East. The ideas of English Liberalism were destined to be permanently influenced by this pamphlet, and thus it came about that the Oriental policy of all Liberal Cabinets in the nineteenth century pursued one and the same line, from Palmerston to Gladstone, up to Grey and Asquith. It is the line of pro-Russianism, the advocates of which were disposed to give Constantinople to the Tsar, and do not hesitate even now to demand that the question of this city should be held in abeyance in case Russia, when once she has recovered from her revolutionary fever, may desire to possess it. Indeed, a certain historian has said, not without some justification, that Tsarism has always manipulated Liberal Cabinets in England as easily as her own.

The best political historian of Turkey and Islam

that Europe has ever produced, David Urquhart, tried at the time to cure European and British diplomacy of the erroneous conceptions which would have imposed upon Turkey reforms that had been elaborated in the Chancelleries of St. Petersburg. He fulminated against the foolish application of artificial formulæ to the East, and made an impassioned appeal for the preservation of good Musulman traditions, of the vitality of which he was convinced. He recommended the admission of Turkey into the European system, certain that, if constant foreign interference in her affairs could be prevented, she would become once again an exceedingly useful and prosperous element in the balance of power, and would be able to play a splendid part in carrying on her historic rôle as the advanced guard of Western knowledge in Asia. Between 1830 and 1878 he preached absolute non-intervention on the part of the European Powers in Turkish affairs, in order that the historical process of transforming the Moslim peoples into modern nations might be accomplished on natural lines with the collaboration of enlightened Westerners familiar with the problems of the East and free from all diplomatic intrigues. To entrust the initiative and the carrying out of all reforms to the accredited representatives of science, instead of making it a weapon in the hands of diplomatists, is one of the soundest pieces of advice he gave to the Powers, and it holds good to this day. Urquhart was the first to realize that the Near East question, in the form in which the detractors of Islam presented it to public opinion in Europe, was merely a mystification, which was bound to lead to massacres. Western diplomacy has never understood that the essence of the problem lies in producing a fundamental change in the relations between Europe and Asia, by allowing a noble religion and valiant races to solve the vital questions of their existence unmolested by external intrigues.

The Europeans, whom Lord Byron had called " a race that buys and sells," paid but scant attention to the dramatic conflict between Tsarism and Islam. The problem was never enunciated in its universal and human aspect, and international intrigues continued to serve to hasten the catastrophe of a world war. It is probable, however, that the Christians of the Near East would have been the gainers in the end, if, instead of clinging to their privileges and going half-way to meet foreign intrigues which they all too frequently provoked, they had co-operated with the movement of reform which was shaking Islam.

III

After the Congress of Paris (1856) Russia invented a system which simply meant the suicide, limb by limb, of Turkey. The plan of fostering the antagonism between Christianity and Islam, and of preventing by subterranean methods, the application of the principles of conciliation, professedly supported before public opinion in Europe, was an adroit policy all the more certain of success as the theocratic elements in Turkey were for a long time opposed to progress. If the Tanzimat, the first great attempt at reform in Turkey, ultimately failed, this was largely due to muddled foreign interference. To accustom the Christians of the Near East to constant interference from abroad and to a system of incessant meddling, amounting to a regular tutelage over Islam, was to give them *carte blanche* against the Turks. Beaconsfield thought the Musulmans as worthy of participating in the work of modern civilization as they had participated in the powerful civilizations that had preceded our own. He wished this country to preside, in brotherly collaboration, over the economical education of the Moslim peoples, and over the vast movements which have been agitating the minds of Musulmans for the last hundred years. Unfortunately England, which was soon to be absorbed in domestic troubles in which Gladstone was to play a high-handed part, did not understand Lord Beaconsfield. Hatred of Islam was, as everybody knows, one of the strongest actuating motives of Gladstone, deeply impregnated as he was by Christian theology. Under his ill-omened influence, the Eastern policy of Great Britain changed completely, and she became, in fact, the unconscious ally of Tsarism against Islam. Instead of becoming the impartial though benevolent mediator between Christianity and Islam—a task clearly indicated by the Asiatic interests of the Empire—the latter turned ever more and more towards the Tsarist standpoint, whose one object was to blot out from the political system of the world the very real, though stationary, forces which Islam still holds at her disposal. It was thus, in this fatal direction, to which the failure of the first constitutional movement presided over by Midhat Pasha seemed to lend some justification, that England was plunged headlong when, after her moral isolation subsequent to the Boer War, she saw rising before her the spectre of German expansion. When, on the one hand, the forces of Reaction in Turkey had recovered under Abdul Hamid, and had thereby aroused the unanimous hostility of Europe against Islam, and on the other, the fear of Germany haunted all minds in England, public opinion in this country began to grow accustomed to the favourite idea of Tsarism, and applauded Edward VII. when he went to Reval to meet Nicholas II.

The Turkish Revolution of 1908 once again upset all the calculations of European diplomacy. Its popularity in England forced the Foreign Office to reverse its engines and to open a fresh credit on behalf of the Turks. The latter now turned with enthusiasm towards their English friends, because they were convinced that their salvation depended upon Great Britain and not upon Germany, who, for thirty years, had protected Abdul Hamid and had extorted onerous concessions from him in return. The way in which the British Ambassador was received in Constantinople after the restoration of the Constitution throws a brilliant light upon Turkish hopes in 1908. Here was a wonderful opportunity of realizing the ideas of David Urquhart. Chance had once again offered England the friendship of a progressive Moslim nation ; it was a matter of saving the world from a universal conflagration which was smouldering under the cinders of the Near East problem—to save it by educating the Moslim peoples politically and economically, and by reconciling the races which were tearing each other to pieces on the borders of Europe and Asia. Unfortunately for Europe, the narrow theological spirit of Gladstone had supplanted the wide humanity of Beaconsfield in the direction of British policy, and the vicissitudes of party politics had entrusted the disciples of the former with the duty of keeping in touch with the National Movement in Turkey during this critical and decisive period of the Turco-European drama.

In these circumstances, the Turkish Revolution of 1908 was bound to fail in its attempt to reconcile so many different and frequently conflicting interests.

European diplomacy took advantage of the grave errors which inevitably occur in any work of reform and revolution in the Near East, in order to resume its policy of destruction with an alacrity which contrasted all too conspicuously with the long and magnanimous patience it had exercised towards the autocratic system. And thus the Revolution of 1908 foundered on the rocks of the Balkan War of 1912. The Turks, finding no reliable support in Western diplomacy, threw themselves blindfold into the arms of Germany, after having made fruitless attempts, both in 1913 and 1914, to secure British collaboration in the work of reform in Asia Minor. Thanks to private initiative, however, this collaboration was offered to the Turks in certain circles in England where they had preserved friends sincerely desirous of contributing to the revival of Asia Minor. Men with the highest administrative gifts and organizers who had proved their worth in South Africa and Canada declared themselves ready to undertake the task of reorganizing Asia Minor for the Turks, with that Anglo-Saxon tenacity which constitutes the strength of the race, and has contributed to its greatness in all continents. These Englishmen, who were unconsciously inspired by the generous spirit of David Urquhart and who responded enthusiastically to the idea of restoring the ancient soil of Islam to modern culture, instead of subjecting it to a selfish Imperialism, approached the Foreign Office, a few months before the Great War, for its consent. They received no encouragement.

And thus another opportunity was lost of reviving the understanding between the British Empire and the Moslim world, on which depended the peace, not only of the Near East, but possibly of the whole world. Under the pressure of German expansion, England preferred the friendship of Tsarism and sacrificed that of Islam. When a miracle relieved England at one blow of both pan-Slavism and pan-Germanism, by sweeping away the Hohenzollern and the Romanoff Empires, a unique opportunity once more lay open to her in the Near East. The horse on which the heirs of Gladstonian diplomacy had laid their money had broken its neck, whereas the so-called Sick Man, though still staggering under the final blows of the War, declined to be laid in his grave. The Turkish National Movement, which had blossomed like an indigenous plant in Asia Minor, suddenly confronted Turkey's grave-diggers with a vigour which once again proved that it was impossible to reckon on the Near East, without taking into account the race that ruled it.

The question was whether, at this decisive moment in the Near Eastern drama, a world-wide power like the British Empire—one of the mightiest pillars of which rests on Asia—could afford the luxury of regarding the Moslim world through Greek orthodox optics, of wishing to impose a Greek doctrine upon Islam, and of being actuated by prejudice, when all she was asked to do was to replace her British glasses on her nose in order to contemplate matters from an exclusively British point of view, and to shake herself free from Levantine influences, hardly in keeping with the central interests of the Empire. During the War, purely peripheral and ephemeral interests may have united to produce the illusion that the power created by Venizelos and Zaharoff might usefully replace the anti-English forces gathering behind the wings in Europe in the new balance of power in the Mediterranean. The idea of substituting a pro-English Greece for Turkey in the Eastern basin of the Mediterranean, and of combating the anti-English tendencies in the Near East by setting up the Greater Greece of Venizelos and Zaharoff to oppose them, has always been an impossibility owing to the fact that Greece was very far from possessing the capacity of playing such an important rôle so far beyond her political, military, and financial resources.

Why is it that England persisted in that way in spite of the events between 1920 and 1923? In order to answer this vexatious question it would be necessary to examine two matters with which I can deal but cursorily here. In the first place, it forms part of the programme of the Anglican Church to become united sooner or later with Greek Orthodoxy, with whom she has been flirting for over thirty years;

indeed, theological disputations worthy of the Middle Ages were arranged between the two Communions, the first of which took place in the episcopal palace of Archbishop Eulogus of Russia before the War, with the object of trying to reconcile the dogmas of the two Churches. Although the grand design of ecclesiastical union was not fulfilled, as neither of the two disputants would consent to sacrifice one iota of their dogmas, a tactical alliance, at least, was achieved in the shape of a common programme of religious policy uncomprisingly directed against Islam. To seize Constantinople and make it the seat of that future Union of the two Churches which had always been flashed in the eyes of the English Episcopacy by the clever diplomatists of Greek Orthodoxy—such was the immediate political object of this interesting intercommunion. That is why Lord Robert Cecil and his brother, the militant protectors of this Orthodox-Anglican programme, were always to be found in the van of those who wished to exterminate the Turks. That is why the Archbishop of Canterbury and the Bishop of London, the Bishop of Manchester, and their brethren were always ready to preach a crusade against Turkey and Islam. And that is why Mr. Lloyd George and his Nonconformist brethren persisted with such stubbornness in their efforts to kill the Turkish nation.

The political and economic autonomy of Islam was contested by a diplomacy which, at the Congress of

Versailles, as well as at Geneva, accepted the negroes of Haiti, but refused to receive the Ambassador of the Emir of Afghanistan in 1921 and the Envoy of Mustafa Kemal Pasha in 1922, treating them as inferior creatures. Is it possible to trace in these incidents the unconscious reflection of an intolerant and aggressive religious policy well aware of what it is doing? If this is a possible assumption, it is a strange phenomenon indeed for our time.

The second consideration to which I referred consists of the selfishness of a powerful body of merchants and commercial people who imagine that Asia was invented purely for their material advantage, and that her sole function in the world is to serve as a milk-cow, providing dividends for the great Companies, whilst the Asiatic is nothing more than a beast of burden, to be exploited. It is these tradesmen who have turned the British Empire, whom her founders intended to be the hearth of a grand spiritual idea, into a distributing office for dividends. It is they who were always opposing the economic organization of the world upon the new basis of co-operation, of co-partnership within an international community, based upon mutual respect and profit, and benefits shared in common. The Anglo-Saxon genius, which invented the spiritual idea of a Commonwealth of Nations, has fallen a victim to a group of narrow-minded, intolerant, and selfish individuals, greedily grabbing at every surplus profit that can be realized on earth or in heaven. And yet, the true profit of the Empire, her consolidation, and her spiritual vocation, as conceived by the greatest thinkers of England, would consist in definitely furnishing the proof that she is useful, nay, indispensable to mankind without distinction of race or creed. Humanity yearns to be organized, yearns to create organic bonds between the peoples that compose it. The British Empire might long ago have played, and may even yet play, this great part in the life of the world, but on one condition only—she must adopt as quickly as possible an honest policy towards Asia, and especially towards the Moslim world. And the attitude of the British Government towards the Turkish nation will be the first criterion of such a policy.

IV

Ever since the Turks inherited the rulership of the Near and Middle East from the Khalifs of Bagdad and Cairo, they have always formed the advanced guard of Islam. And from the very beginning they have always been faithful to the spirit of tolerance bequeathed to them by their ancestors. The very existence of so many foreign institutions within their Empire for generations is a sufficient proof that narrow nationalism is not an invention of their race.

Europe is consequently all the more surprised to find them forming a National State out of the remains of their Empire. But the idea of nationality is the logical consequence of European teaching: if the Turks are turning to account an idea in the name of which they were constantly attacked throughout the nineteenth century, it would surely be unfair and disgraceful to cast in their teeth certain artificial traditions of Islam, at the very moment when they are trying to free themselves from such trammels in order to return to the purer ideals of their religion and of their race. Turkish nationalism is in the process of drawing practical conclusions from the education it has received from Europe; and yet, this is the very moment chosen for reproaching her for doing precisely what Turks have been asked to do ever since the Charta of Gulhane of 1839. For the proceedings at Angora since November, 1922, constitute the greatest political impulse given to a fundamental reform that Musulman institutions have received since the Tanzimat.

The reformation of Islam has already been attempted in various spheres. In the domain of religious philosophy, in jurisprudence, in morals these attempts date back to the Mou'tazilites, the rationalist school of Musulman thought in the eleventh century. Islam has never ceased to be in a process of transformation. But the reforms attempted by various Musulman sects, sincere though they may have been, were only rarely able to produce any lasting practical results. To purify the faith and the creeds, to correct the customs, and to raise the moral tone of certain primitive peoples in the East, was the aim of a whole host of thinkers, heads of Moslim Brotherhoods, marabouts, or simple believers. But the forward march of Islam required something more. For a fundamental reform of Musulman institutions to have the faintest chance of becoming universal, two essential conditions were prerequisite : firstly, that it should not take place under Christian pressure ; secondly, that it should be inaugurated by a strong, energetic, and independent Moslim nation.

These two conditions are to-day fulfilled by the Turks. The reformation of Musulman institutions can only come from a Musulman nation whose prestige stands intact in the eyes of all followers of the Prophet, and whose independence is guaranteed by her own power and her own will. Those who assert that Islam is bound to dogmas, and that every attempt stands condemned which would endeavour to free her from stereotyped traditions unsuited to the exigencies of world economics, forget that the theory of an immovable Islam has always been untenable, and that Islam has frequently been shaken by historical convulsions of thought. Her jurisprudence, which the Turks are reforming to-day in accordance with modern political science, has for many centuries revealed the influence of Roman Law. Even her dogma is ear-marked by Hellenistic thought, whilst her philosophy has incorporated neo-Platonic and Indian ideas. The receptive character of Islam has been unequivocally demonstrated by the greatest Orientalist of our time, Professor Goldziher, in his celebrated *Lessons on Islam.* Goldziher has shown that Islam has proved her capacity for organic assimilation and the utilization of foreign elements throughout her whole history. It is wrong, he maintains, to hold Islam responsible for those moral imperfections and signs of intellectual stagnation which are really caused by racial proclivities and climate. From the moral point of view, Islam is still a world-wide empire worthy of every consideration on the part of thinkers; but between doctrinal Islam and the Islam of history there are infinite shades of possibilities, and her future development depends precisely on the attitude adopted towards her by Turkey.

Among the Musulmans the Turks are the political race *par excellence.* From the time that they supplanted the Arabs as the Rulers of Islam they have been able, for a long time successfully, to play the part of intermediary between East and West. Turkey opened the doors of Asia to Western civilization long before Japan. In every domain of human activity she formed a bond of union between the two continents by merging both hemispheres together through the mixture of races, of which the Ottoman Empire has been the stage ever since its foundation.

Goldziher, whose scientific authority is unanimously recognized, says that "The elevation of the Ottoman Empire to the rank of a first-class power in the world of Islam succeeded in ousting the intolerant Hanbalite cult ever more and more, in the territories submitting to its rule, whilst the influence of the Hanafite system (to which the Turks belong) increased in proportion." Indeed, it is sufficient to glance at the organic statutes granted by the Turks to the Christian communities at the time of the Ottoman Conquest to prove that their tolerance in matters of religion was exemplary and surpassed that of the European races at the same period.

The prophet himself said: "Difference of opinion in my community is a manifestation of divine mercy." Ample sectarian development followed this saying of Mohammed: the freedom allowed to the exposition of religious doctrine was the characteristic feature of Musulman thought in the first centuries of the Hegira. The common sentiment of princes and people, says Sir Thomas Arnold, has generally condemned intolerance on the part of professed theologians. The recognition of a common God is put forward in the Koran as the basis for friendly relations with the followers of rival creeds. "Dispute ye not, save in kindliest sort, with the people of the Book," said Mohammed. "Let there be no compulsion in religion," is another saying of the prophet.

This is the clearest injunction of toleration, and in harmony with the injunctions of the Koran, Mohammed wrote a letter to the bishops, priests, and monks of Najrân, promising them the protection of God and His apostle for their churches, and freedom from disturbance or any interference with their rights, so long as they remained faithful to their obligations. He permitted the Jews, in Medina, to practise their own faith, until their implacable hostility led to their expulsion from the city, and he gave instructions to Mu'adh Jabal, whom he sent on a mission to Yaman in the year 10 after the Hegira, that he was not to compel any Jew to abandon his religion.

When Arab rule was extended into Persia, it was averred that Mohammed had given directions that the Zoroastrians were to be treated exactly like the "Ahl al-Kitab," the "People of the Book." There is even an account of a Mohammedan general (in the reign of Mu'tassim, 833–42) who ordered an *imam* and a *mu'adhahin* to be flogged because they had destroyed a fire-temple in Sughd and built a mosque in its place. In the tenth century, three centuries after the conquest of Persia, fire-temples were to be found in almost every province. Even the Manichæans survived as a separate sect until the end of the tenth century, owing to Moslim toleration. In the reign of Ma'mun, Yazdanbakht, the leader of the Sect, held a public disputation with the Moslim theologians in Baghdad.

In India, after the Musulman Conquest, though during the later period there was a considerable destruction of Hindu temples, the settled Mohammedan Governments appear often to have respected the State endowments granted by the former Hindu rulers to religious foundations, as was done in the case of the temple of Brahmanabad in the province of Sind, where Mohammedan rule was first established in India. The same tradition survives in present Mohammedan States in India, such as Haidarabad and Bahawalpur, which still assign revenues for the support of Hindu temples.

The non-Moslim living under a Mohammedan Government was styled a "*dhimmi*" (*lit.*, "one with whom a compact has been made"), and the conditions under which he lived were supposed to be regulated by the agreements made with the Moslim conquerors as they extended their dominion over various cities and districts. The theory was that the *dhimmi*, in return for tribute paid and in consideration of good behaviour, received protection from the Moslim Government and immunity for life, property, and religion. The prophet said: "Whoever torments the *dhimmis*, torments me." And, in his testament, the Khalif Omar thus addressed his successor: "I commend to your care the *dhimmis* of the Apostle of God ; see that the agreement with them is kept, and that they be defended against their enemies, and that no burden be laid upon them beyond their strength." In a like spirit, the Turkish code ordains that the *dhimmis* are not to be disturbed in the exercise of their religion. In the first centuries of Moslim rule the various Christian Churches enjoyed a toleration and a freedom of religious life such as had been unknown for generations under the Byzantine Government. This is the conclusion of Sir Thomas Arnold, who devoted his life to the study of Moslim history.

In the course of the long struggle with the Byzantine Empire the Khalifs had had occasion to distrust the loyalty of their Christian subjects, and the treachery of the Emperor Nikephoros was not improbably one of the reasons for the harsher treatment initiated by Harun Al Rashid (786–809), who ordered the Christians to wear a distinctive dress and give up to Moslims the Government posts which they held. But the prescriptions of the jurists and theologians who interpreted the Koran were often more intolerant than the actual practice of the Government. Don Leone Caetani, the great Italian historian of Islam, has proved that the early conquerors had no power to enforce the cruel principles of Abu Yusuf, Harun Al Rashid's great jurist, and historical facts prove that the true spirit of Islam was not always forgotten by the later

Moslim Governments. In the sixteenth century, the majority of Moslim jurists held that the *dhimmis* (Christians and Jews) should be treated with kindness and consideration and not with contempt, when they came to pay the tribute. A powerful influence in the direction of toleration in a period when feeling against the Christians were very bitter, and when the disorder in Mohammedan administration made their position more precarious and exposed them to the tyranny of local officials, was the extension of the religious thought in which devout Moslims found consolation for the misery of the time.

The practice of Mohammedan Governments, says Sir Thomas Arnold, seems, generally, to have been, to leave to each separate protected community the management of its internal affairs, and to permit the religious leaders to administer the laws as to marriage, inheritance, etc., in accordance with the ordinances of the particular faith proposed by the persons concerned. An important testimony to the toleration of Moslim rule is the fact that persecuted Christian and other sects took refuge in Mohammedan lands, to enjoy there the undisturbed exercise of their several cults. The persecuted Spanish Jews at the end of the fifteenth century took refuge in Turkey in very great numbers. The Calvinists of Hungary and Transylvania and the Unitarians of the latter country long preferred to submit to the Turks rather than fall into the hands of the fanatical House of

Habsburg. The Protestants of Silesia in the seventeenth century looked with longing eyes towards Turkey, and would gladly have purchased religious freedom at the price of submission to Moslim rule. The Cossacks, who belonged to the sect of the Old Believers and were persecuted by the Russian State Church in 1736, found in Turkey the toleration which their Christian brethren denied them.

The conclusion of Sir Thomas Arnold may be accepted as an impartial historic truth: "Of toleration in the Musulman world generally it may be said that it was more operative in the earlier centuries of the Hegira than in the days of the decline of the Khalifate, or in modern times when the pressure of Christian Powers exasperated Moslim feeling. The civil government has, as a rule, been more tolerant than the clergy, and the regulations of jurists have seldom been put into force with all their rigour; though practice has varied with time and place, the persecutions that have occurred have been excited by some special and local circumstances rather than inspired by a settled principle of intolerance." The favourable judgment of Gobineau on Islam is, on the whole, justified by the facts of history. The Koran never allowed any tyranny over conscience.

As regards the attitude of Turkey, intolerant theocracy was an importation into Asia Minor and had nothing to do with the soul of the Turkish nation. It is well known that the ancestors of the Turk, Djenghiz Khan and Timur, Mongols and Tartars, were originally free of religious fanaticism, and that the great Khans attended the ceremonies of all religions, the value of which to the State they fully realized; that the great Emperors of India, all of whom were of Turkish stock, were real free-thinkers in the sixteenth century, and that one of them, Akbar, a pure Turk, dreamed of the formation of a synthetic religion in which the Madonna, whose image had been brought to him by some Portuguese monks, would have played a prominent part. The various branches of the Turkish race, which provided emperors and statesmen for three continents, from China to the South of Russia, played an historical part similar only to that of the Romans and the English. The empires they founded served, as did the Roman Empire, as intermediaries between several systems of civilization and were for a long time the principal agents of communication between Asia and Europe. The British Empire itself is only their more fortunate successor in certain parts of Asia, inheriting the mission which has left such a deep mark on the history of the Turks, who acted as the organizers and administrators of that immense continent long before the British Empire emerged from the chaos in the East, in the seventeenth and eighteenth centuries.

V

Powerful economic interests, connected with the raw material problem in the East, have forced the Turks to reorganize and to reconstruct their social, judicial, financial and economical institutions, their agriculture as well as their general methods of production. This is the task which the reformers of Angora have set themselves. To judge them from a distance of over three thousand miles, without thoroughly examining the motives of their actions, is all the more foolhardy inasmuch as those who condemn them have committed and continue to commit the grossest errors in circumstances far less complicated and in the midst of a firmly-rooted civilization.

The peasantry of Anatolia know nothing about theological subtleties. In order to understand their state of mind, in order to judge of the human material, so to speak, which lies behind Mustafa Kemal, it is necessary to turn to analogous historical situations, such as that created by Koszciuszko and Kossuth. The former was backed by the peasants of Poland, the latter by the Hungarian peasantry who knew nothing about international political combinations; and yet both men fell victims to such combinations. It is not surprising, therefore, that Mustafa Kemal, who knows history, and whose country has proclaimed the principles of the American

Revolution of 1776 for Islam, has no desire to share their fate, but prefers to follow in the footsteps of Washington. He refused the Khalifate, which was offered to him by members of the Grand Assembly of Angora, and preferred to declare that the Khalifate is embodied in the principle of Republican Government.

The recent decision of the Grand Assembly of Angora to expel the Turkish Imperial Family has just reopened the fundamental problem which interests Musulmans all over the world. Since the fight for independence started by a handful of Turks in 1919, on the morrow of the Greek landing at Smyrna, Islam has been in ferment. The occupation by the Allies of the seat of the Khalifate, the complete foreign grasp on the holy places of Islam have powerfully contributed to that ferment, of which the beginning dates back to the first Balkan War, in which the Moslims discovered for the first time what they call Europe's betrayal of them. It was then, only, that a Moslim delegation from India came to Europe, under the leadership of Mohammed Ali and Syed Wizir Hassan, to protest to Sir Edward Grey, then Secretary of State for Foreign Affairs, against the abandonment of the Turks by England. When, in December, 1912, Mohammed Ali made his first appearance in London as the delegate of the Indian Moslims, a great number of members of both Houses surrounded him at the banquet sporting the Turkish colours, where he made his speech proclaiming the solidarity of Indian Moslims with Turkey. I remember being impressed when, under the chairmanship of the Hon. Aubrey Herbert, M.P., the official delegates of the Indian Moslims began their political banquet with a prayer for the Sultan-Khalif. The loyalty of Indian Moslims to the British had of old been a favourite subject of discourse for many writers; the creator of the Imperial Crown in India, Lord Beaconsfield himself, regarded Islam as the pillar of the Anglo-Indian system. This suddenly discovered solidarity between Bombay and Stamboul, proclaimed in London in 1912, surprised the English greatly, though historians should remember that Indian Moslims helped the British Government in 1857 against the revolt of the Cipayes, because the Khalif of Stamboul advised them to do so. The solidarity of Islam remains uncomprehended in this country till this day, although Mohammed Ali returned to the charge in 1920, going so far as to demand an audience of the Pope (who received him better than Mr. Lloyd George), and endeavouring to get in touch with the Sorbonne in order to make the best in Europe understand the motives which impelled him to espouse the cause of Turkey.

The world was no less surprised when the Grand Assembly of Angora proclaimed, on March 3rd, the final downfall of the House of Osman, suppressing by one stroke of the pen the old and time-honoured conception of the personal Khalifate. For years the

Indian Moslims have reproached their British rulers with undermining the position of the Sultan-Khalif, by making common cause with the Sultan's enemies. A member of the British Cabinet, Mr. Montagu, was led by a solemn telegram from the Viceroy of India to raise his voice in favour of the Khalifate, and fell as the result of an indiscretion in March, 1922 Two years later the Turks themselves got rid of an institution which had existed for six centuries, and was for so long the rallying point of the Sunni world. The Powers who tried to get possession of the moral and political control of the Sultanate of Stamboul by opposing it to the Angora movement, are perplexed by this phenomenon of Musulman psychology and scent in it a new chance of regaining the sympathies of the partisans of a temporal Khalifate.

For centuries, European unanimity in favour of the Christians of the Near East, and against the Turkish nation in particular, seemed assured. The theory which prevailed and was more or less gratuitously propagated by superficial or too passionate observers of Islamic life and doctrine, was that Islam is an enemy of human progress, and that there is nothing to be hoped from the Turks, nor from Moslims in general, from the standpoint of modern science. According to this theory, every attempt to replace the Moslim States by formations either Christian or controlled by Christians, ought to be welcomed. Those who, for reasons of toleration, forgave the Moslims their religion, concentrated their disdainful judgment on the Turks, who, in their opinion, ought to disappear as a nation to make room for a state less refractory to exterior ambitions. It was in the name of so-called modern ideas that the Turks, probably the most maligned and most hated race in history, were thus condemned.

I have no space here to retrace the historical genesis of that ferocious sentiment of Turcophobia which is revealed in most Anglo-Saxon speeches, whether from the lips of Mr. Lloyd George, or of a head of the Anglican or Nonconformist Church. In the eyes of those who *know* the East, the massacres do not suffice to explain it ; for irrefragable evidence has proved that the Christians of the Levant have borne a very active part in these massacres. Besides, the history of every people abounds in such regrettable incidents, which simply remind us how erroneous is the theory of philosophers and poets deifying humanity—that mere phenomenon of political zoology. Certainly, passions, evil as well as sublime, have played their part in Near Eastern events, but the history of the real moral responsibility for the racial and religious strife of the last century has not yet been written in an impartial and scientific manner.

Here we can indicate some of the factors which have helped to bring about the dangerous antagonism which sets the West and the East by the ears. Among such factors the theologians of both hemispheres are in the foreground, while economic appetites, more or less avowed, are wrapped up in beautiful humanitarian theories for the benefit of simpletons.

The theologians who have got hold of the Eastern problem seem to me the victims of a politico-religious literature, little calculated to advance the hour when the moral union of mankind would permit the noblest aspirations to be realized. In the Moslim East, the artificial theological explanations of the Khalifate problem have nothing to do with the original teaching of Mohammed. During the first centuries of Islam freedom of thought and of discussion was considered as the very basis of the Musulman attitude.

If anything could reassure the modern world as regards the intentions of Turkey, it is precisely the downfall of the autocratic system in the East. After the fall of the Hohenzollerns, the Romanoffs, and the Habsburgs, that of the Sultans is historically logical. It is the end of an old and obsolete formula of Oriental absolutism. It is a great impulse to the future reforms, which must be elaborated quietly after peace has been restored in the East as a whole. But it is important that henceforward the world should remain neutral and objective in this fight of the new Musulman moral forces against the old formulæ. It is important that nobody should lend aid to the Moslim reaction against the Turks, who this time truly represent a sincere effort to adapt their institutions to new principles.

The Grand Assembly of Angora, that renovation of the old Turkish assemblies, called " Kouroultai," is certainly not the last stage of Turkish evolution. It must not be judged by isolated gestures, but as an original attempt to restore the vote to the people in a country which, in half a century, has seen a tyrant, a weak-minded man, and a traitor succeed one another in the seat of Mohammed the Conqueror and Suleyman the Magnificent. An immense revolutionary process has been opened in Islam, and we see only the beginning of it. Let us wait and watch.

What we know for certain is that the teaching of Islam is not opposed to what is happening. The eternal conflict between the principle of free discussion and the principle of theological bondage is starting again.

Some Moslims of the old school will cry out Atheism! and accuse the Turks of impiety. Let us remember that the Treaty of Sèvres, which was signed and accepted by the Turkish Imperial family, contained the following clause:

> " Turkey renounces formally all rights of suzerainty or jurisdiction of any kind over Moslims who are subject to the sovereignty or protectorate of any other State."

" No power shall be exercised directly or indirectly by any Turkish authority whatever, in any territory detached from Turkey or of which the existing status under the present Treaty is recognized by Turkey." (Section III, General Dispositions of the Treaty of Sèvres, Article, 1394.)

Not one member of the Turkish Imperial family ever raised his voice against this clause. Not one member of that family ever offered his services to the National Army of Turkey. Not one of them joined Angora in order to suffer and to struggle with their own people. It was Mustafa Kemal Pasha who cancelled this clause from the Treaty of Lausanne.

Quite apart from this, the elective principle is at the very foundation of Islamic institutions, of which the power of adaptation to modern political science is contained in the principle of *Idjma,* the consent of the majority of Moslims to any new proposal. " The principle of Idjma," says Goldziher, " contains in germ the faculty for Islam *to move and evolve freely.* It offers a timely corrective to the tyranny of the dead letter and of personal authority. It has proved, at least in the past, the principal factor in Islam's capacity for adaptation. What might not its continuous application in the future bring to pass? "

Driven to choose between the principle of Idjma and stereotyped theological authority, between the reform of Musulman institutions by a fresh national agreement and the maintenance of an institution fallen captive to foreign influences, the Turks have overthrown an artificial tradition which has never had the pure Islamic doctrine on its side. The old and dramatic dilemma, which so long paralysed the evolution of Islam, has once more been stated. Is it the moment for enlightened Moslims or Westerners to weaken the Turks who have at last given, of their own initiative and without foreign pressure, the great impetus to Islamic reformation ?

From the standpoint of pure Islamic doctrine all new ideas are perfectly compatible with the teaching of Mohammed, if they have the approval of the Idjma. The principle of Idjma, says Goldziher, signifies that " that which is accepted by the whole Moslim community as true and right should pass as such. All that has the general approval of the followers of Islam is right and claims to be recognized obligatorily, and it is right only under the form which general approval, called the *consensus* of opinion, gives to it. . . . The only valid doctrinal authorities are the men and writings recognized as such by the general sentiment of the community, and that not in Synods and Councils but by an almost unconscious *vox populi*, which in its collectivity is held to be infallible. The Khalifate should be conferred upon the most worthy by the general voice of the community."

We see now what are the principles which the Turks can invoke to justify their action which has opened the problem of the transmission of the Supreme Imamat. Certainly, Angora claims to find the solution of the problem in its own sphere of influence. It is on that point that the discussion in the Moslim world will be concentrated. Already voices are making themselves heard from all the horizons of Musulman thought acknowledging Angora's moral right to govern this immense debate, after having beaten the Byzantine enemy.

VI

There is nothing in the true spirit of Islam of which a good European cannot approve. Mr. Ameer Ali, himself considered as a leading *Mu'tazilite*, which means a rationalist, explained, in his beautiful book on *The Spirit of Islam*, why the School of Freedom of Thought was defeated in the eighth century of the Hegira by the reactionaries among the Moslim theologians. He gave a really impressive and dramatic description of the formidable struggle between the ideas of progress and the principle of unchanging authority which convulsed Islam from the tenth to the fourteenth centuries, and ended in the triumph of rigid dogmatism, in spite of the original instructions of the Prophet. Mr. Ameer

Ali's present opinion appears to me as being in contradiction with the conclusions of his standard work, in which he made the most powerful appeal to the progressive forces in Islam to reconsider the whole position of the Moslim world and to return to the original teaching of Mohammed, whose views are thoroughly in conformity with the principle of free criticism. I am surprised to see Mr. Ameer Ali now advocating a dogmatic interpretation of the Khalifate problem, instead of asking simply for a new examination and a new discussion before he pronounces his verdict.

The fact that stands out most conspicuously from Mr. Ameer Ali's standard work is that the tenth century (the fourth of the Hegira) was the tragic century *par excellence* for both Europe and Asia. It has certainly always seemed to me the most fateful period in the destiny of mankind, in the sense that all our problems, all our racial questions, came into being at the time of the great migrations. Mr. Ameer Ali confirms my point of view, whilst enlarging upon it considerably. At a time when the continent of Europe was torn by material desires exclusively, by the animal needs of the races which in the tenth century fought for the pasture lands and the habitable portions of the only temperate climate known at the period, the continent of Asia, which had already been prepared by Islam and was in a full state of intellectual fermentation, was the theatre of a similar conflict, but with this special difference, that she was, to a greater extent, involved in a battle of ideas connected with the problem of Good and Evil.

Whilst Europe was tearing herself to bits in order to get something to eat, Musulman Asia, in a high state of civilization, witnessed the birth of a religious and philosophical struggle regarding the true meaning of the Prophet's message, on which the *Mu'tazilites* and the partisans of rigid dogmatism could not come to any agreement. The rationalistic school demanded a modern interpretation of the Prophet's teaching, and took up their stand on the obviously contemporaneous nature of some of his precepts, laying down as a principle the individual responsibility of each man, and his capacity for judging between good and evil, and of allowing himself to be guided in the right road by God, through the medium of an act of free moral choice. The followers of this philosophic and religious thesis became very numerous after the foundation of the School of Medina, but according as Islam conquered different races possessing but little of the spirit of tolerance, a rigid dogmatism laid hold of the newcomers Musulman rationalism ended in complete defeat after a struggle of four centuries.

Mr. Ameer Ali traces the principal phases of this tragedy of the soul of Islam, and proves irrefutably how Islam was paralysed in her spiritual evolution by fanatical races who entered the Musulman fold with a hereditary bias wholly in favour of rigid dogmatism. The finest minds, the greatest thinkers of Islam between the tenth and the fourteenth centuries were on the side of freedom of thought; even those who, like the great mystic, Al Ghazzali, preferred contemplation to action. Al Ghazzali, whilst opposing philosophic rationalism, peremptorily rejected fanatical dogmatism and called fanatics false friends of Islam. In the name of human thought, he combated the Mollahs and the retrograde theologians with sublime and altogether modern arguments. But this Pascal of Islam involuntarily contributed to the defeat of science in the Moslim East. Those who exploited the ignorance of the multitude turned the general tendency to contemplation to account, in order to kill the spirit of freedom and action.

A formalistic scholasticism thus took possession of Islamic teaching from the fourteenth century onwards, that is to say, from the very moment when, in Europe, scholasticism was in its death agonies, and modern science was taking its first steps in the West. The controversy between Abu Hanifa and Ibn Hanbal resulted in a dogmatic theology which ended by sterilizing in Islam that scientific spirit, the dazzling splendour of which still amazes all students of the Musulman sciences of that time: geography, medicine, mathematics, astronomy, philosophy flourished at Cordova, Sevilla, Bagdad,

Basrah, Damascus and Cairo. Mr. Ameer Ali gives an imposing list of the great scientific figures and the great intellectual discoveries of Islamic culture, and certainly no serious investigator in Europe would dare to contradict this statement to-day, when in Spain a great Catholic scholar, two years ago, discovered the Musulman sources of the greatest Catholic poem—the Divine Comedy of Dante. Unfortunately, both for Asia and Europe, the authority of factitious ecclesiastic traditions weighed down the Musulman world, which from the time of the European Renaissance played little or no part in the evolution of science. As in medieval Europe, the cause of freedom of thought succumbed before the ecclesiastical principle.

Several centuries of intellectual sterility followed upon the result of this conflict. European historians, and with them the majority of Persian, Arab, and Indian historiographers, have been accustomed to attribute this to a race whose military virtues made them masters of Asia for many centuries. Mr. Ameer Ali himself is not always innocent in this respect, either in his *History of the Saracens* or his *Spirit of Islam*. How, then, can we expect European scholars, such as Professor Edward Granville Browne or Professor Margoliouth, to have escaped this one-sided attitude, when they found themselves under the spell of the numerous Musulman civilizations which they made the object of their admirable erudition. They saw only one aspect of the relations between the Persian or the Arab people and the race which I have called the most calumniated in history. History lays the ruin of Islamic civilization at the door of the Turks. In spite of a few facts which lend this assertion a certain semblance of truth, this accusation has no foundation in history. For if these facts, taken alone, seem incontestable, their bearing and their connections appear to have been too little studied and badly interpreted. This historic verdict on the Turkish race is open to revision.

It has been asserted that she has created nothing, done nothing, and produced nothing in the course of a long political and military domination. But, in the first place, are people aware of the conditions under which the Turks, the founders of powerful States in China, in India, and the interior of Asia, entered into history? It is true that the Turkish race has never excelled in the domain of abstract thought, at least as regards originality. But if the right to a national existence depends upon the originality of the abstract ideas of a race, some of those who hold a high position in Europe would find themselves in a precarious situation. Different rôles are allotted to different races and nations in accorddance with their special aptitudes, and a great man of action has never been reproached for having produced nothing in the domain of literature or art. Looked at from the international point of view, the rôle of the Romans, to whom the Anglo-Saxons are so often compared, resembled that of the Turks far more closely than is generally supposed. Roman thought and Turkish thought have this in common, that they were both directed towards political action, and only considered art from the point of view of pleasure. Just as the Romans drew their ideas from Greek and Egyptian sources, and adapted them to their needs and to their own level, so the Turks adopted the Persian, Arabian, Chinese, Indian and French civilizations with which they came into contact. They played the part of organizers and governors in several continents just as the Romans did ; on another system and with other methods, it is true, and in an entirely different human setting ; but, nevertheless, they played their part for a long time successfully, and it was thanks to their expeditions that the various civilizations of Asia and Europe met and knew each other, with the result that a synthetic Musulman culture came into being, which is still developing, and will only be completed if Western civilization, which has made its appearance in Asia through the French and the English, gives it efficacious, generous and practical aid.

What Turkish Islam requires is modern education and science. She must be freed from the sterile scholasticism and the archaic formulæ of her intellectual life. The abolition of the Sheriat, and the introduction of modern scientific schools in Asia Minor serve this purpose. Those who maintain that the Turks are, of all the Moslim races, the least amenable to intellectual reforms, are the victims of an error which has been spread abroad by the numerous candidates who, for over two centuries, have coveted the Turkish heritage. On the contrary, a mentality but little suited for imaginative metaphysical speculations, such as the eminently practical mentality of the Turks, is the only one in Islam that can easily detach itself from old theological formulæ, and take up the task of reformation, on condition that Turkey is left to her own initiative. The alleged fanaticism of the Turk is a figment of European and Byzantine invention. For never has any race been more docile towards the teachings of toleration than the Turk, when he was allowed to give up following the foreign Mollahs who came to Turkey to preach metaphysical subtleties. Like every other religion, Islam adopted a fanatical form in cases where the races converted to it possessed fanatical natures. Religious fanaticism in Turkey was an accidental product, the responsibility for which does not lie with the Turkish nation, in spite of the testimony of only too many bloody pages in her history, which are rather due to political and social causes. Remember the observations made by Renan on the ethnic causes of Semitic fanaticism.

VII

It is important that we should comprehend the problem which confronts us. Islam, which was, at its origin, a small religious community at Mecca, and a primitive political organization at Medina, became a world empire, founded at first on military prowess, like the so-called Holy Roman Empire, afterwards, when the great Moslim States crumbled, upon a very elevated sentiment which makes of the Musulmans the greatest human confraternity in the world. That which unites the human races in the eyes of Mohammed, is the sense of the dependence of them all on the one God. Listen to the Koran :

> " Do not separate. Remember the benefit of God towards you. For aforetime you were enemies, but now He has bound your hearts so that you are become brothers."

These noble exhortations were long countered by the ancestral customs of the primitive peoples who followed the Prophet, and Islam became a religion of feudalism like Christianity in the Middle Ages, simply because feudalism then prevailed in the East as in Europe, and the lords of Moslim territories adapted the religion to the requirements of their cause. The principle of Cæsaro-Papism was imposed on Islam by Zoroastrian influences, at the accession of the Abbassides to the Khalifate. Turkey put an end to this conception of the Khalifate. Do not encourage the opposition of the bigots ; do not play the game of the religious die-hard party in Islam ; that is the wish I form for those who are responsible for the Moslim attitude. Islam has hardly passed the theological phase of its development, and a host of social and economic conditions are still needed to make of it, or rather make of it again, a religion of equality of all men, in accordance with the true spirit of the Prophet.

For that purpose the Turkish nation possesses one great advantage: she knows from experience what it costs a proud people to allow itself to be lulled to sleep by old-fashioned theologians. Turkey has suffered more than any other nation in recent history, and she has developed a will of iron, and a national conscience. She even possesses one virtue that Europe has lost since the time of Napoleon: the Turk knows how to obey his recognized leaders. In St. Helena, Napoleon expressed his regret at not having had Turks under his command, instead of Europeans. To-day the notion of the Chief exists nowhere except in Asia. The Turk above all has this idea bred in the bone, and he devotes himself to the man who commands him, when once he is convinced that the Chief has been sent by God, and is a father of his people. What a magnificent virtue which might long since have been turned to the advantage of Europe in Asia, if the West had only understood the value of an honest alliance with the Turk!

The Turkish standpoint as to the Khalifate is nothing more than a new proposal which should be discussed and should serve as an impetus to the revival of Musulman thought. The downfall of the Turkish dynasty is nothing more than an historical and political incident, which, instead of exciting blind passions and prejudices, should induce the Moslim world to reconsider calmly the foundations of Islam, and to put away any theological bias based on preconceived judgments.

Mustafa Kemal, who organized and directed the greatest movement which ever succeeded in the East since the partition of Moslim territories among Western Powers, who rules the only independent and modern Moslim State now existing, and who rules it owing to the immense services he rendered to his people, should have a fair hearing before Moslims who judge him from the point of view of the future of Islam. His opinions should have more weight than the opinions of those more or less short-sighted theologians who had opponents even in their own day, and who, moreover, knew nothing about the needs and sufferings of present-day Islam, having, of course, died long ago. Sectarians who lived in past centuries cannot suppress the elementary right of every Moslim of examining afresh the fundamental truths, as well as the essential interests of the living generation of Islam. For Islam was originally and essentially a religion of human freedom: Moslims are only bound to Allah, and they need no intermediary between the Almighty and themselves.

I consider the Turkish point of view as inspiring an attempt to return to the original teaching of Mohammed. Listen to the Koran: "You will believe, you have to obey Allah, and those among you who command." Mawerdi, one of the greatest scholars of the Sunni world, defined the qualifications of the Khalif as follows: the Khalif has to mobilize the Musulmans for the defence of Islam; he has to administer justice to the Moslims; and he has to protect the holy places of Islam. Now, the Grand Assembly of Angora consider themselves as the highest expression of popular sovereignty. The Turkish Republic was proclaimed with a view to administering justice to the Turkish nation. Two of the essential duties of the Khalifate are consequently in the hands of those who represent the Turkish people; as regards the principal duty, the mobilization of the Moslim army and the protection of the holy places, the Turkish point of view is that it would be a mystification to let the Moslim world believe that Turkey would be, in the near future, in a position to repair the terrible wrong done by King Hussein of the Hedjaz when he joined the enemies of Turkey.

Turkey is determined to work for her own salvation

first; and to develop a strong and conscious Turkish nation on modern scientific and economic lines. And Mustafa Kemal's opinion is, as it appears from his speech of March 1st, that the Khalifate is now vested in the Turkish Republic as a whole, in its fundamental principle of national sovereignty. The Turkish army, however, could not be mobilized for any other purpose than the defence of that sovereignty.

The Musulmans outside Turkey should also work first for their own salvation, instead of quarrelling about the interpretation of old sectarian texts, which contain controversial matter. Sectarian interpretation of the Khalifate controversy may be the source of grave dangers for the moral unity of Islam. The only standpoint from which Moslims should consider the political position of the Moslim world is the standpoint of the supreme moral and intellectual interests of the living generation of Islam. The Prophet never considered himself as infallible: he always admitted his own errors as a human being. Why should Moslims accept some sectarian of the past or the present as a supreme and infallible authority? Why refuse to the greatest living man in the Moslim East, to Mustafa Kemal, the right to give a new interpretation of the *Ikthalaf*, the science of controversy? Why should a true Moslim consider the brain of those who talked or wrote for Islam, as a higher source of authority than the brain of Mustafa Kemal, who conceived and carried out the fateful action which has saved the dignity of Islam in the last five years? For Mustafa Kemal and the Grand Assembly of Angora with the peasantry of Anatolia have been the saviours of the dignity of Islam to-day, while those who pretend to give advice to Angora from London, or to condemn the Turkish Republic, have been tamey acquiesing, or enjoying themselves in Europe.

Why should the Moslim world refuse to take into consideration the standpoint of a Moslim nation which suffered and died while others talked and talked again? Why should a great historical movement, like the Turkish, have less authority to interpret the original teaching of Islam than any private individuals?

I will go further: The whole world is in a chaotic state. Tremendous events await the Moslim world in the next ten or twenty years. Islam may play its great rôle once more. Western and Central Asia, a good part of India, and North and Central Africa are under the spiritual rule of Islam. A great genius is wanted for the sake of the next generation; a genius who understands the causes of the present weakness of Moslim nations, as well as the real significance of what is happening in the whole world; a genius who is prepared to give an example to Asia as to how she could adapt herself to the new conditions of world economics, to modern science and technical knowledge. If Mustafa Kemal and the

Turkish nation agree to take up this great duty and to transform their people into a Commonwealth of a newly-modelled Moslim State, based on the original teaching of Mohammed, in accordance with the science of our time, every enlightened Moslim thinker should help them, instead of favouring the reactionary forces which inspire the Sectarians.

The continuance of the anti-Turkish propaganda signifies that the world persists in meddling in a *moral question* vital to Islam, in putting spokes in the wheel of Islamic evolution. If enlightened Moslims in their majority would accept the standpoint of Turkey with regard to the Khalifate, if Mustafa Kemal were accepted as the real leader of modern Musulman thought; if deep in the Moslim soul, the Idjma, the decision has already been made to confer upon Angora the right to direct the reformation of Musulman institutions, and to interpret the Khalifate in accordance with the new social and spiritual aspirations of Islam, let us bow before the choice of the Musulman *élite*, and do not let us play the game of the ignorant crowds. Let us rather work with that *élite* for the revival of Asia, instead of fighting against them in the name of superannuated prejudices. Equilibrium for the world and repose for mankind, the very object of Islam, as well as of all great religions, depend on it.

One word more: the fundamental quality of the Eastern soul, as it appears in Eastern history, has been always to accept a great genius. If Mustafa Kemal proves to be a constructive genius, no Moslim and no Westerner should block his way.

THE PROBLEM OF EGYPT

Lord Milner, in his Report on the Special Mission sent by the British Government to Egypt after the Egyptian Revolution of March, 1919, wrote the following significant words: "We have never honestly faced the Egyptian problem, and our neglect to do so is in a measure responsible for the present situation." This confession on the part of a great British statesman emboldens me to ask my readers to search their consciences and to examine the Egyptian question from the moral, judicial, and, above all, the psychological point of view, and to allow me to lay particular stress upon certain aspects of the problem. For the diplomatic history of the question, interesting though it is from the international standpoint, will only occupy our attention in so far as it helps us to understand the human and psychological side of the relations between England and Egypt.

I

The problem of Egypt may be examined from two different standpoints. The first, which is the one hitherto adopted by British statesmen with regard to the whole of the East, consists in examining the map of the world primarily from the strategical point of view and noting the central position upon it of the valley of the Nile, which, as a matter of fact, is so essential for the military defence of the British Empire; of noting, too, the fundamental fact of the existence of the Suez Canal, which joins together three seas and three continents, and the importance of which for the trade routes of the Empire cannot be exaggerated. And in thus examining the map with the eyes of the strategist, it is easy to see that the valley of the Nile provides a magnificent military base, an excellent requisition area, and a wonderful source of revenue, in short, a fine colony to exploit. Anyone who considers merely this aspect of the problem, if he is a Briton and wedded to obsolete militarist formulæ, will certainly say to himself: "What madness to abandon the valley of the Nile, to surrender it to the unknown, to jeopardize our communications with the Dominions and with India, and to allow other Powers to hatch intrigues against us." The mind thus imbued with military formulæ, thinking only in military terms, and regarding the rest of mankind as an army on the march, which must be crushed if he is to survive, will never accept the idea that spiritual and moral guarantees can possibly replace strategic safeguards.

The second point of view—the one which I myself

adopt—consists in continuing to examine the problem without forgetting the importance of the tremendous strategic value of the Nile regions, but also bearing in mind the nature of the peoples that inhabit the great trade routes of the Empire. For, after all, the valley of the Nile is something more than a military base or a fortified camp from which to dominate the Suez Canal and the Red Sea. The valley of the Nile is inhabited by human beings who, while they may differ from ourselves in many respects, are yet of the same flesh and blood, and have a soul uplifted by the same desire for better things and moved by that universal tendency characterizing the mysterious forces hidden away in the depths of human nature, in every latitude and in every age. And if one can only realize that a whole multitude of human beings—about fourteen million Egyptians—are to be found in this fascinating valley, anxious to be transformed into a modern nation, seeking the ways and means for that transformation, trying hard to adapt themselves to world-wide economic conditions and to Western science, marching ahead, going wrong sometimes perhaps, but determined at all costs to awake from their lethargy, holding out their hands to the West and begging it to give them the chance of free development in accordance with their spiritual and material needs—and if one can only incline onself towards the soul of the Eastern peoples, one cannot help perceiving that new methods of statesmanship are required to solve the vastly complicated moral problem involved in the question of the future relations of England and the whole of the Western world with the peoples of the East.

II

The problem of Egypt, indeed, is but one link in the fateful chain of problems with which humanity is faced, and the solution of which will determine the future of the whole of the Western world, including England. Nowhere is it possible to see with greater clarity the sometimes disastrous results of the conflict between Western ideas and the ancient customs of the East, or to gain such a curious confirmation of the fact that the world is advancing to a new order. The central position of Egypt has no merely strategic significance : for Egypt, together with Turkey, of which she formed a part until 1914, also forms the spiritual pivot of the Eastern question. Nevertheless, the historic changes which are taking place under our eyes in the valley of the Nile require some explanation.

There is no need for me to describe to you how Mehemet Ali, the first Viceroy of Egypt, conquered the valley of the Nile, and how he gave the first impetus towards a new development through opening up Egypt to Western influence, by inviting European experts, and more especially Frenchmen, to help in the creation of the whole apparatus of modern armaments, modern schools, public works, and irrigation, which have placed Egypt in the position which was her due in the political and economic balance of power in the basin of the Mediterranean. You all know the reasons for which England and Russia made war on Mehemet Ali who, at the time, was regarded as an instrument in the hands of France, and why the great Powers prevented him from dethroning the Imperial dynasty in Turkey. We know, in fact, that Mehemet Ali wished to regenerate the Moslim East, and dreamed of placing himself at the head of the Ottoman Empire and infusing it with a new life. But the Tsars were anxious to prevent the regeneration of Islam, in order that they might reap the benefit of the troubles following on the weakness of Turkey ; and England helped Russia for tactical reasons, convinced that Mehemet Ali would not be such a supple instrument in the hands of her diplomatists as the degenerate family which still kept up a semblance of power at Stamboul. Unfortunately, the fact that Mehemet Ali was surrounded by French technicians, and followed the inspiration of French ideas of reform, provided a certain basis for the suspicion that he was merely a tool of French expansion.

The study I have made, however, of this interesting period of diplomatic history has imbued me with the most profound conviction that once again English diplomacy made a mistake. Mehemet Ali only asked for, and accepted, French collaboration in the regeneration of Egypt because the other Powers refused their help, and because England at that time—as in 1914 with regard to Turkey—was on the side of Tsarism, the mortal foe of the East. For the same reasons as the Turkish Revolution of 1908 was forced into the arms of Germany, that is to say, because it had no true friends elsewhere in the West, the Egyptian Revolution of 1839 turned to France, who was ready to seize the opportunity. We know that the army of Ibrahim Pasha, the son of Mehemet Ali, was standing at the gates of the Taurus, when the veto of the great Powers put a stop to his victorious advance. Mehemet Ali was obliged to submit to the verdict of the so-called Concert of Europe, and to content himself with the Viceroyalty of Egypt, to which the Sudan was afterwards added. The Convention of London of the 15th July, 1840, and the Firmans of the 13th February and the 1st June, 1841, defining the relations of the Sultan and the Khedive, settled the status of Egypt in the framework of the Ottoman Empire, the suzerainty of which was nominally safeguarded.

But the apparent triumph of the Sultan had been dearly bought by his diplomatic and moral dependence upon the Tsar, who had saved the throne of Stamboul, thanks to the support of Lord Palmerston. The fifteen thousand Russian soldiers who occupied Buyukdere, on the Bosphorus, and the Treaty of Unkiar Iskelessi (1833), which, in a barely disguised form, established a Russian Protectorate in Constantinople, showed that the Ottoman Empire had become the slave of its so-called friends. The cause of the East—of Turkey, as well as of Egypt—was lost. For Mehemet Ali, although he was by nature a despot, would have given a great impetus to the revival of the whole of the Moslim East if he had not been prevented from carrying out his policy. The fact that he shook the Mohammedan East and awoke it from its long stupor, remains to secure for him his place in history.

The mark that Mehemet Ali left on Egypt raises a philosophical question, which I shall not attempt to answer. It is the question whether the French political and social ideas, which invaded Islam a century ago and succeeded in undermining its most sacred traditions, answer to the fundamental needs of the Musulman soul, as it had evolved during fourteen centuries. We have only to consider the facts; and the influence of French revolutionary ideas in the Near East, is a fact which is still operative in its spiritual evolution, and which we must bear in mind if we wish to arrive at just conclusions.

III

Egypt, as a self-governing State, made wonderful strides during the period immediately preceding the British occupation. The financial extravagance of the khedive Ismael form but an isolated incident among the more important events which characterized the economic evolution of Egypt between 1840 and 1882. The great irrigation schemes date from this period. The railways of Egypt, the sanitary works of Cairo, the formation of the beautiful gardens of Ezbekieh and Gezirah, the Zoological Gardens, the gradual transformation of Old Egypt into a country of comfort, in fact, all that is called modern civilization, including the founding of the first schools of Western learning, were the work of an autonomous and practically independent Egypt: for the Sultan of Turkey never interfered in the administration of the country. The dams near Cairo, the drainage works for the improvement of agriculture, and a large number of radical measures, aiming at the development of economic life, prove that there existed in Egypt a conscious desire for the creation of a modern state when, after the bombardment of Alexandria by Admiral Seymour, General Wolseley made his appearance upon Egyptian soil.

It is generally known that the alleged reason for

the British occupation was to be found in the chaos of the khedival finances, a disorder which created further disorder among the masses of Egypt, who groaned beneath the charges levied upon them. The Anglo-French financial control, called the Dual Control, had been established for several years when the famous revolt of Arabi Pasha broke out. The true history of this movement is not even yet sufficiently understood. But one thing is clear: and that is, that the Egyptian people, led by the students, among whom was to be found the future Zaghloul Pasha, then Saad Effendi Zaghloul, demanded a Constitution and succeeded in obtaining a Parliament, which put an end for a moment to the autocratic rule of the khedive. The British occupation stopped this movement, and in the month of September, 1882, General Wolseley declared that his sole intention was to re-establish the authority of the khedive, and that British troops would retire from Egyptian soil as soon as order was restored. This solemn promise was repeated seventy-three times during the period of occupation by responsible statesmen in Great Britain . among others by that celebrated moralist, Mr. Gladstone, by the great Lord Salisbury, by Lord Rosebery, Lord Dufferin, Lord Granville, Sir William Harcourt, Sir Charles Dilke, Joseph Chamberlain, etc., etc., all of whom most emphatically declared that the Egyptian question involved the honour of England, and that a Protectorate or annexation would seriously compromise her fair fame.

All this forms part of diplomatic history, from which I am borrowing a few instances without wishing, however, to emphasize their importance. But more significant than these instances, more significant even than diplomatic notes, is the fundamental and all-important fact that the real reason for the British occupation was to be found, not in the constitutional movement of 1882 in Egypt, nor in the wish to re-establish the fallen authority of the Khedive, but simply the existence of the Suez Canal.

The opposition of Lord Palmerston to the construction of the Suez Canal is well known. He considered the French scheme menacing to the defence of India, and to British interests in the Mediterranean. When Lesseps obtained the concession from the Khedive, Said, in 1854, British diplomacy did everything in its power to prevent its being sanctioned by the Sultan of Turkey. The conflict lasted until 1866, when the Firman legalizing Lesseps' concessions was granted. Later on, in 1875, Lord Beaconsfield induced the Rothschilds to buy up the shares of the Suez Canal Company, which were held by the Khedive, amounting to a total of 85,506 shares. These, together with the shares which had already been acquired by Great Britain, meant that 176,602 out of 400,000 were in the hands of that country. Lord Beaconsfield gave a spicy account of how he succeeded in forestalling France in the purchase of the shares of the Khedive, who was obliged to part with them in order to meet his debts. Lord Derby, who was then Foreign Minister, proposed a reorganization of the Suez Canal Company by transforming it into a sort of syndicate, headed by the representatives of all the maritime powers. It can readily be understood that the British Government was opposed to the existence of a monopoly in foreign hands.

Thus the Suez Canal became a matter of capital importance in British policy. In 1877–8, at the time of the Russo-Turkish War, England protected the Canal against all interference from Russia. In a despatch sent by Lord Derby to Russia on the 6th of May, 1877, it was solemnly declared that England would regard a blockade of the Canal " as a menace to India, and as a grave injury to the commerce of the world."

In consequence of the Revolt of Arabi Pasha against the Khedive, Italy suggested that an international police force should be formed ; and Turkey was ready to accept the suggestion. But the Powers failed in their efforts to combine, with the result that France, having refused to participate in a military action, Sir Garnet Wolseley landed British troops in Egypt. There they have remained for forty-two years.

IV

The details of the debarcation, the ultimatum addressed by Admiral Seymour to the Commandant of the Alexandrian forts, which were so antiquated that they could not possibly be regarded as a serious menace to the European fleets, assembled in the Bay of Aboukir, the protestations of Egypt, and the international complications that ensued, have only historical interest. The one fundamental fact that is obvious to the eyes of any impartial observer of the chain of events in 1882, is that the British occupation could boast of no legal basis whatever before the bar of history or of international law. This is no fanciful consideration, and it must not be supposed that it has no legal value. The almost complete unanimity of European jurists, and a whole list of authoritative works on the law of nations, have questioned the British diplomacy which led to the state of affairs of 1882, regardless of the international Conference summoned at Therapia on the 23rd July, 1882, the deliberations of which were interrupted by the roar of the British guns bombarding Alexandria, although it had been agreed that no isolated action was to be taken whilst negotiations were pending. The Institute of International Law had, in 1879, drawn up a programme of recommendations for the safeguarding of the freedom of the

Suez Canal. These recommendations, which were based upon the Clayton-Bulwer Treaty of 1850, were entirely ignored. I shall return to this later on, as it deserves the attention of the League of Nations in connection with the future of the Suez Canal.

Egypt was obliged to submit to violence, in spite of her constant protestations to the world. But the world was busy over its own petty concerns, and gradually grew accustomed to the *fait accompli* of the presence of a British army on Egyptian soil. They acquiesced the more readily inasmuch as the British control of the khedival Government looked like progress in the eyes of those who do not believe that Orientals are capable of self-government; and the fact that European trade did not suffer in any way, sufficed as far as the outside world was concerned. For merchants all over the globe are only too ready to make light of the freedom of a distant country if they can see their way to reaping profit from the established system, whatever it may be; and thus Egypt was reduced to a new form of political slavery—a veritable miracle on the part of the genius of compromise.

V

A few hundred English officials laid down the law to the Egyptian people, although every Government Act bore the signature of an Egyptian Minister, acting in the name of the Khedive. This imposition of British rule upon native authority, the semblance of which was rigidly observed, in order to prevent the Fellah from realizing that he was being governed by the foreign power, has often been admired as a masterpiece of modern diplomacy. But I do not think it is possible yet to pass any definite judgment upon its intrinsic worth ; for the final consequences of an important step can only be perceived after several generations. Nevertheless, I should like to point out that, from the moral point of view, nothing could have been more unfortunate than the confusion created by the sudden introduction of English ideas into a nation profoundly influenced by another current of Western culture, a country that was, as yet, too little advanced in modern learning to be able to stand such a spiritual shock. If English ideas had penetrated Egypt through spiritual channels at the beginning of the nineteenth century, before the rule of Mehemet Ali, it is possible they might have done some good in giving a certain direction to the Musulman soul. But coming, as they did, after more than fifty years of French intellectual influence, and introduced, moreover, by force, they did more harm than good. They threw the soul of Islam into confusion and completed the great moral evil that the West has inflicted upon the East in snatching it by violence from its own religious traditions.

The harm is done. The West has tried to kill the

East morally, politically, and socially. In the case of Egypt, the indirect method of controlling the Government down to the smallest details resulted in demoralizing the Egyptian nation, though Egyptian finances were put on a sound basis. The class which at that time constituted the nation—the Effendi, at least, was merely a tool in the hands of the British officials. Circumstances facilitated for a long time the task of controlling affairs. For the Egyptians, with very few exceptions, bowed their heads until the voice of Mustafa Kemal, their first national leader, began to revive once more, in the breasts of the *élite* gathered about him, the idea of human dignity.

The spiritual consequences of the British action, which put an end, in 1882, to the constitutional evolution of Egypt, became but slowly apparent, whilst the material benefits to which British diplomacy pointed, in order to justify its action, were not regarded as unmixed blessings by everybody. The Fellah, accustomed for six thousand years to working for a master, who exploited him without compunction, bowed before the English inspector, as he had bowed before the Bey, or the tourist who gave him a penny. The ease with which the Fellah was governed created in the English mind a false illusion of absolute security. And this illusion gave birth to the idea that anything was permissible with regard to these unfortunate creatures, the Fellaheen.

VI

The Great War seemed, at first, to justify this illusion. Egypt not only accepted without a murmur the rupture of her time-honoured connexion with the Sultan of Turkey, but the Government contributed both economically and financially to the War against Turkey. On December 18th, 1914, the Protectorate was proclaimed. An Egyptian Labour Corps was formed in which over one million Egyptians were enrolled, with a promise of excellent treatment and exceedingly good pay. Lord Milner himself pointed out in his famous Report that the first signs of discontent on the part of the Fellaheen were due to the fact that the Labour Corps was frequently ill-treated, and that the promise to employ them only on work behind the lines was not kept. Clearly the Fellah had reached the limit of his patience. The commandeering of cattle, the brutality of inferior officials, and insupportable humiliations did the rest. When Zaghloul, who is himself the son of a Fellah, and proud of the fact, put himself at the head of the national movement, the whole of Egypt became united in the transport of feeling, which ended in placing him, after the incredible events of the last five years, in the seat of Prime Minister.

English public opinion, as a whole, is still ignorant of the truth concerning the national movement in

Egypt ; it knows but little of the deep causes underlying it, of its constructive programme, its leaders, and its inner meaning. From the very beginning a by no means disinterested campaign was inaugurated to distort the aims of Zaghloul, to depict him as an extremist agitator, a dangerous intriguer, and an inveterate enemy of the British Empire, ready to ally himself with any foreign power in order to slake his hatred of England. Never has a more crafty calumny been so transparent as this theory regarding the extremist aims of Zaghloul Pasha.

Imagine a man who has attained a patriarchal age ; who has served the Egyptian Government for some forty years as Counsel in the Court of Appeal, as Minister of Justice and Public Instruction, as the chosen Vice-President of the Legislative Assembly ; a man who won the esteem and sympathy of Lord Cromer, a man who worked prodigiously in order to fill the gaps in his Azharian (purely Moslim) education by the study of the French language and French law when he was forty years old ; a man who had acquired a knowledge and experience of affairs to which Lord Cromer rendered homage in his book on Modern Egypt ; who had a brilliant career as a self-made man, as a lawyer and as a statesman. Could such a man turn extremist, all of a sudden, for the mere pleasure of taunting his former friends ; could he break off laborious negotiations in London with regard to the future of Egypt, for the sheer joy of being deported to the Seychelles at the age of seventy? No. The truth is far more complicated, or, if you will, far more simple. But in order to unfold it I must call to my support certain facts in the history of the five years during which Mr. Lloyd George and Lord Curzon swayed the destinies of the East.

VII

If Egypt submitted apparently without a murmur to the proclamation of the Protectorate in December, 1914, if she seemed to resign herself to a war-time measure hastily decided upon, in order to meet the exigencies of the moment, it was because she trusted the solemn promise contained in the telegram of His Britannic Majesty to the Sultan of Egypt, who had succeeded the dethroned Khedive, in which it was declared that the rights of Egypt would be safeguarded on the conclusion of peace, and that her independence would not be overlooked when the right moment arrived. This promise was repeated in the proclamation of General Maxwell, the Commander-in-Chief of the British Forces in Egypt, in the following terms:—

"Great Britain is now fighting to protect the rights and liberties of Egypt, which were originally won upon the battlefield by Mehemet Ali. . . ."

On the day after the Armistice, or, to be more precise, on the 13th of November, 1918, Saad Zaghloul Pasha, the elected Vice-President of the Egyptian Legislative Assembly, the meeting of which had been postponed by the British Authorities in Cairo, presented himself with two of his colleagues before Sir Reginald Wingate, the High Commissioner of England for Egypt, and respectfully asked for passports to London, as the representatives of a National Delegation appointed to discuss the problem of the future relations between England and Egypt, in conformity with solemn pledges made in 1914. But let me give you Lord Milner's own words. I will quote them verbatim:

"On the 13th November, 1918, Zaghloul Pasha, with two other leaders of the advanced Nationalist group, paid a visit to the High Commissioner and expressed their desire to go to London in order to put forward a programme of 'complete autonomy' for Egypt. Simultaneously, the Prime Minister, Rushdi Pasha, proposed that he should himself, together with Adly Pasha Yeghen, the Minister of Education, proceed to London to discuss the affairs of Egypt, a plan which he stated had the full approval of the Sultan. The contention of these Ministers was that the Peace Congress would give official consecration to the Protectorate, and that, therefore, its nature could not be left undefined. Under the Turkish suzerainty, Egypt had had certain rights, and they desired to know what their rights would be as against Great Britain under the Protectorate."

"Sir Reginald Wingate reported these proposals to

the Foreign Office, and was informed in reply that 'no useful purpose would be served by allowing Nationalist leaders to come to London,' and that the visit of the two Ministers would not be 'opportune' at that moment. The Foreign Secretary explained that, owing to the fact that he and other Ministers would be absent from London in connexion with the Peace negotiations, they would 'not be able to devote sufficient time and attention to problems of Egyptian internal reform.' Rushdi Pasha . . . tendered his resignation. . . . It would appear that, in spite of the insistence with which the High Commissioner appealed for their reception, the real urgency of dealing with the Egyptian problem at that critical moment had not been realized."

So much for the opinion of Lord Milner.

But what are we to think of a statesman charged with safeguarding the supreme interests of a great and powerful empire at a most critical moment who, with one sweep of the hand, without reflection and without weighing the psychological and political consequences of his gesture, refused to perform an elementary act of courtesy not only towards an old Minister, the friend of Lord Cromer, but also towards the Government of a whole country which had rendered invaluable services to England? For Lord Allenby himself had declared that, without the services rendered by Egypt, victory would not have been won in the East in 1918. I am emphasizing the historic responsibility incurred by Lord Curzon through his categorical refusal, until 1921, to discuss the Egyptian problem with the Egyptians, because

I know that the tragic events which followed upon the action of the noble lord are misunderstood in this country and are always quoted as proofs of the Egyptian nation's anti-British feeling.

The facts, as they may be deduced from the correspondence of the leaders of the first National Delegation (called the "Wafd"), with the British Residency at Cairo, prove the moderate policy of Zaghloul Pasha. This Delegation consisted of twelve members under the Presidency of Zaghloul, and its object was to place the aspirations of Egypt before the world. On account of a petition addressed on the 3rd of March, 1919, by the "Wafd" to the Sultan, Sir Milne Cheetham, then acting High Commissioner, decided, with the approval of his Government, to deport Zaghloul Pasha and three other members of the "Wafd" to Malta. This was the signal for the revolution. Disturbances broke out on the 12th of March at Tantah; the provinces of the Delta joined the conflagration on the 14th and 15th of the same month. British troops were attacked, soldiers and civilians were murdered, and telegraphic and railway communications between Cairo and the Delta, as well as with Upper Egypt, were cut off. By the 18th of March the provinces of Behara, Gharbia, Menufia, and Dakhalia were in open revolt. Upper Egypt was entirely isolated. On the same day a crowd of fanatics at Deirut killed two British officers and five men, as well as an inspector of prisons. On the 26th of March repressive military measures culminated in a stabilization of affairs, with the result that the chief lines of communication were reopened.

Lord Milner, who gives an impartial account of the facts I have just cited, adds :—

> "Thus, within a week from the deportation of Zaghloul Pasha and his associates, a movement anti-British and even anti-European had assumed grave proportions. It was a national movement backed by the sympathy of all classes and creeds among the Egyptian population, including the Copts."

I agree with the second part of this remark, but my personal experience leads me to say that the first part, ascribing the revolution and the disorders which accompanied it to a hatred of the foreigner, is by no means consistent with the essentially gentle nature of the Egyptian people. The disorders can only be explained as being due to a sort of outburst of hysteria or of rage, to which every nation is prone in times of nervous tension. Primitive people react in a primitive way to an insult offered to the most elementary ideas of human dignity, such as characterized the Eastern policy of Lord Curzon. If you cannot forgive a primitive crowd for a moment of savage despair, what are you to think of those who have had the advantages of an Oxford education and have yet proved themselves incapable of weighing the psychological consequences of their actions?

Lord Milner himself in the following words severely condemns the conduct of Lord Curzon :

" It is obvious," he says, " after the event, that the Egyptian Ministers should have been encouraged to come to London when they proposed to do so, and Sir Reginald Wingate, whose advice on this subject was fully justified by the sequel, would have done well, in our opinion, to urge his views with even greater insistency. After this initial mistake events moved more rapidly in Egypt than the Administration appear to have realized."

A period of exasperation followed the cruel repressive measures, in spite of the liberation of Zaghloul and his colleagues whose departure for Europe was authorized by Lord Allenby, the new High Commissioner, after a general strike lasting three days. Lord Curzon had declared with his characteristic complacency that the Zaghloulites had not the support of the upper classes, and that the official class in particular was perfectly satisfied with the Protectorate. The Egyptian officials replied to this by an unanimous strike, during which the whole machinery of Government was stopped in order to prove to Lord Curzon that Zaghloul had the whole Egyptian nation behind him.

What, during these tragic days, were the aspirations of Egypt? What were the demands which necessitated that famous act of refusal on the part of Lord Curzon, the great expert on the Eastern question ?

VIII

The following is a faithful translation of the text of the *Résumé of Egyptian Aspirations*, as it was drawn up by Zaghloul Pasha on the 14th of December, 1918, with the approval of the National Delegation. It is a document of fundamental historical importance, and can be placed side by side with the famous National Pact of Angora which established the unchangeable principles of Turkish national life.

1. Egypt insists upon securing her independence :

(*a*) Because Egypt has never ceased to demand this independence even at the cost of her children's blood. Her victories would have enabled her to win this sovereignty for herself, had not the Concert of the Great Powers in 1840–41 forced her to reduce her pretentions to a minimum, and to content herself with a liberal autonomy, which, as a matter of fact, very closely resembled complete independence ;

(*b*) Because she now considers herself freed from the last bond which secured her to the suzerainty of Turkey, that country being no longer in a position, owing to the results of the war, to exercise that suzerainty ;

(*c*) Because she considers that the time has now come for her to proclaim a sovereignty justified by racial conditions and her spiritual and material position.

2. Egypt desires a constitutional form of Government ; the details of the régime will be arranged in

accordance with the peculiar situation of the country regarding foreign interests. Economic, administrative, and social reforms will be inaugurated, for the successful accomplishment of which the country will not fail to appeal, as she has done in the past, to the guidance of Western science.

3. Egypt proclaims that the privileges of foreigners will be scrupulously respected, and if experience has shown that some of these privileges can be improved upon, she will, in a liberal and sincerely sympathetic spirit, propose modifications of a kind to secure the progress of the country and to safeguard the interests concerned.

4. She undertakes to examine the establishment of measures of financial control, the efficacy of which, as far as the countries interested are concerned, will not be inferior to that of the measures which preceded the agreement of 1904, and of which the essential instrument will continue to be the *caisse* of Public Debt.

5. She is ready to accept any measure which the Powers may regard as useful for safeguarding the neutrality of the Suez Canal.

6. Finally, Egypt would consider herself highly honoured in placing her independence under the guarantee of the League of Nations, and thus contributing, according to her means, towards the realization of the new ideas of Right and Justice.

(*Signed*) SAAD ZAGHLOUL.

IX

Can any honest thinker tax Zaghloul Pasha with being a dangerous extremist because that brave man dared, in December, 1918, to place the aspirations of the Egyptian nation before the world? Does it require a vast intelligence and knowledge of history and human psychology to realize that such a movement, supported by such an irresistible force of ideas, could not be stopped by a mere wave of the hand, were it even as lordly as that of the great Marquess? Zaghloul has never done anything to menace the legitimate interests of England. The request he made in his letter of the 29th of November, 1918, addressed to Sir Reginald Wingate, was "to confer with the British authorities on the subject of the future of Egypt." He requested this in the name of the nation who gave him his mandate, and he added: "The mission we have undertaken requires our presence in London. We rely upon the traditions of Great Britain. The British have not ceased to give to the world examples of their devotion to the principles of individual liberty. Will not our request for passports receive a quick and favourable response?" And in a second letter, dated the 3rd December, 1918, Zaghloul returned to the charge:

"Our voyage to England has especially for its object only to put ourselves in touch with political leaders, representatives of the nation, and other persons directing English public opinion whose influence on Governmental decisions is undoubted."

And further on :

" The cause that we defend must be presented in the first place to English public opinion, which evidently has need, in order to be enlightened, to receive the details through the natural and authorized representatives of the Egyptian nation."

In a telegram to Mr. Lloyd George, that champion of sacred principles, Zaghloul asked the following question on the 4th of December, 1918 :

" The Egyptians have come to ask themselves whether the principles that the statesmen of the Empire do not cease to proclaim in their daily declarations are applicable to certain fractions of humanity only—to the exclusion of others less favoured ? "

The whole of the East is now asking this primary question not of England alone but of the whole Western world. And that is why, from the psychological and purely human standpoint, the Eastern question throws a significant light upon the mistrust of two-thirds of humanity regarding the honesty of Western civilization. And that is why the spiritual trust of the East in the West, which was so terribly shaken by the policy of Mr. Lloyd George and Lord Curzon, can only be restored *if England herself repudiates the mistakes that have been made and repairs the injuries inflicted, more especially on the races of*

Islam. This constitutes the great problem of moral reparations.

It is impossible to read without profound emotion the letter which Charawy Pasha, late Vice-President of the Egyptian Legislative Assembly, who died three years ago, wrote to Field-Marshal Lord Allenby, just after the revolution of March, 1919, and dated the 29th of March of that year. In it, he begs the High Commissioner to believe that there had never existed in Egypt any hatred of England as a whole, as Lord Curzon had asserted, and that the National Delegation wished to prove to English public opinion "that between the interests of Great Britain and the independence of Egypt a ground of reconciliation was not impossible, but on the contrary easy to find." And he added :

"When the Protectorate over Egypt was proclaimed the Egyptians asked themselves with astonishment how it was possible that with the British, a liberal people, their political situation was worse than with the Turks. . . . The feeling increased before the threats that the young British inspectors addressed to certain notables on the subject of a more humiliating treatment which would be applied when Egypt would be entirely recognized as belonging to Great Britain. . . . During this time the Egyptians were reading with astonishment the news concerning the delegations of other countries: the Hedjas, Armenia, Syria, the Lebanon, etc., which, yesterday, still Turkish provinces, were for the most part in war against the Allies, while Egypt, richer, more civilized, and enjoying already an autonomy guaranteed by an international treaty, had aided in the conquest of these same countries. . . . Then, Egypt alone had no right to have its Delegation, and the Egyptians alone could not go to the Peace Conference to submit their cause, nor could they go to England to appeal to British public opinion. Who would doubt that such treatment could have any other effect than to arouse the anger of the people ? . . ."

After giving a number of proofs of the way in which the Egyptians had been treated both individually and collectively, including a delegation of three hundred Egyptian ladies, who dared to express their sympathy for Zaghloul and the other deportees, the writer of the letter I am quoting concludes :

"What we can assure Your Excellency, with perfect frankness, is, that discontent of the Egyptians is caused by the fact that they are not treated with the same consideration and given the same privilege—or rather, the same right—accorded to small races that are not ahead of them in civilization. All the Egyptians, from the highest to lowest, share this grief. Despair has prompted them to express their sentiment. Everyone expresses it in his own way. Men of authority, officials or private citizens, have expressed it in different written protests ; the youth of our nation has made peaceful demonstrations. As to the inhabitants of the provinces, they have shown how they feel, some by peaceful manifestations, others by different acts of violence, as we know from the official *communiqués*, and some of which inspire in us keen regret."

The historic document which I have just quoted constitutes one of the most important proofs of

Egypt's case. The moral value of such a testimony, although the author of it is dead, is far more weighty than all the assertions representing the "Wafd" and Zaghloul as responsible for the regrettable excesses which provoked Lord Curzon to adopt the attitude he did towards Egypt. The last sentence of it rings out with grandiose dignity: "*To aid a nation,*" Charawy Pasha declares to Lord Allenby, "*is one of the most sacred duties of great men.*"

X

I must at this point render public homage to the uprightness, the frankness and the entirely single-minded character of Field-Marshal Lord Allenby, the British High Commissioner for Egypt. I have the deepest sympathy for the noble English type of which he is a classic specimen, which at once inspires unlimited confidence in its deep and inflexible honesty. He would never have approved of the mistakes made in connexion with the Egyptian question, if he had possessed any profound knowledge of the men and the conditions of the country which he has governed since 1919. But every member of the Near and Middle East Association knows very well that the exclusiveness with which the English live in the East, and which makes very difficult the existence of any friendly relations between Englishmen and Orientals, prevents the majority of British officials from acquiring that psychological insight which would enable them to judge men and things through personal experience. Official experience, class feeling and pride of race are not sufficient and never will be sufficient to lead to any profound understanding of the problem that confronts the West in the East. Moreover, until 1923, Lord Allenby was badly supported and badly advised, but as soon as his staff was improved by being inspired with a more conciliatory spirit towards Egypt, and, above all, since he has had as his principal adviser a man of marked superiority—I refer to Mr. Archibald Clark Kerr, Counsellor to the British Residency—the psychological atmosphere has visibly cleared, and ferocious hatred no longer exists as an obstacle in the way of a reconciliation between England and Egypt.

The second deportation of Zaghloul to the Seychelles and his transference to Gibraltar, whence he returned to Egypt only in the month of September, 1923, require some explanation. It was Lord Allenby who gave the order for this second deportation. But, according to Zaghloul himself and his best friends, the man chiefly responsible for this mistake was Sarwat Pasha, the Egyptian Prime Minister of the day, who hatched a formidable intrigue in order to get rid of Zaghloul, whom he wished to supplant. The facts, as they have been described to me personally, are as follows: Sarwat

Pasha knew that the Residency was in the habit of acting on information sent by the Egyptian Cabinet regarding the safety of the British Colony in Egypt. He accordingly had information sent to the Residency which had only official relations with the Government, that he, Sarwat, could not guarantee the safety of the English in Cairo as long as Zaghloul and the members of the " Wafd " were not deported. His object was to draw up a Constitution to his own liking in the absence of Zaghloul, and so to direct the parliamentary elections in Egypt as to be able, by means of force and corruption, to appropriate to himself all the advantages of the new régime. And he dazzled the eyes of Lord Allenby by making out that he, Sarwat, had the power to guarantee British interests by subterfuge.

Imagine a High Commissioner receiving a Government opinion regarding the menace of Zaghloul's presence in Egypt and of his activity as the leader of the " Wafd " in connexion with the safety of his fellow-countrymen ! It goes without saying that, believing in the honesty of Sarwat, he asked permission from Lord Curzon to have Zaghloul deported to the Seychelles. A High Commissioner who never received any Egyptians except Ministers and high officials, who had no other source of information or other opinions at his disposal than the information and opinions of individuals who, jealous of the great moral power of Zaghloul, were only watching for an opportunity to do him some injury, could have chosen no other course than the one dictated by the most elementary ideas of prudence for the safeguarding of his fellow countrymen. By assuring Lord Allenby that Zaghloul was responsible for the murder of Englishmen in Egypt—an assertion which was an odious calumny—they succeeded in banishing Zaghloul from his country for eighteen months.

I had the good fortune of making the acquaintance of Field-Marshal Lord Allenby on the 20th of February, 1922, in London, when the High Commissioner was here on a visit in connexion with the abolition of the Protectorate. He had been a week in England and had succeeded, under the threat of resignation, in securing the Declaration of the 28th of February from the reluctant fingers of Lord Curzon and Mr. Lloyd George. It was a hard struggle, and I know that Lord Allenby pleaded the cause of a reconciliation with Egypt with all the fervour he could in the circumstances.

On that day, when I had the honour of talking for over half an hour with the High Commissioner in the intimate atmosphere provided by the cosy fireside of an English home, I tried to persuade Lord Allenby that a frank and straightforward conversation with Zaghloul would have done more to prevent misunderstandings than all the equivocal information received at second hand. Lord Allenby replied that he was a friend of Egypt (in his own way, naturally) and that he had tried to meet Zaghloul before the conflict between the Residency and the "Wafd" had become so bitter, but that Zaghloul would never consent to have himself registered at the Residency and that consequently he had never seen the National leader.

A little while ago, when I saw Zaghloul Pasha again in Cairo, on the 1st November, 1923, after his triumphal reception on his return from exile, I asked him the following question: "How is it that you never had any dealings with Lord Allenby during all these critical years?" His reply was that he had never received any invitation or heard any suggestion that Lord Allenby wished to meet him. The only explanation I can give is to suppose that Lord Allenby was waiting for Zaghloul to come to see him of his own accord, whilst Zaghloul was expecting an invitation. At all events, I can only say that Zaghloul Pasha assured me himself that he would never have refused to see a competent Englishman, that his object was always to negotiate with the English, and that in 1919, and at any time since then, he would eagerly have seized any opportunity if it had been offered to him of having a friendly talk with Lord Allenby.

To-day, at last, the High Commissioner can talk openly with the National leader, who is now Prime Minister of Egypt, and I am certain, from my knowledge of the Eastern soul, that Zaghloul Pasha has shaken Lord Allenby warmly by the hand, and that no trace of bitter feeling any longer exists between them.

But what, I ask you, are we to think of the bureaucratic method which required the sacrifice of five years and a number of lives on account of a mere misunderstanding, which could have been cleared up in five minutes if these two men, though fighting each other in support of the supreme interests of their respective countries, had met in 1919 like two gentlemen who respected the rules of the game?

XI

The game is still being played, but its rules are not always observed. In certain circles in England people are still lending an ear to the calumnies of which Zaghloul and the Egyptian nation have been the victims since 1919.

The Encyclopædia Britannica, in one of its new volumes (Vol. 30, p. 943), recognizes that "in justice to the Egyptians it should be recorded that, whatever anticipations had been raised among them as to the outcome of the War, they bore with patience and goodwill the unwelcome disabilities which it entailed, and laid Great Britain under obligations both moral and financial." The point of view of Lord Curzon on the "necessity of maintaining the King's Protectorate" over Egypt proved impossible, in spite of President Wilson's recognition of it, which almost coincided with the first journey of Zaghloul Pasha and his associates, interned at Malta, to Europe. Their efforts to obtain a hearing at the Peace Conference were thus disappointed.

After the failure of the Milner Mission, whose task was to inquire and to report on the form of the constitution which, under the Protectorate, would be best calculated to promote peace in Egypt, the British Government was obliged in 1920 to open negotiations with Zaghloul, who reached London with seven other delegates on June 7th of that year. After deliberations which extended to the middle of August, the general lines of an eventual settlement were drafted. But Zaghloul and his friends were not prepared to commit themselves to acceptance without reference to their supporters in Egypt, and four members of the Delegation accordingly returned to Cairo with a memorandum outlining the bases on which an agreement might subsequently be framed. This memorandum, which came to be known as the Milner-Zaghloul Agreement, was in general accordance with the conclusions adopted by the mission in Egypt, though it went somewhat further, especially as regards the right of Egypt to foreign representation. A letter handed to Adly Pasha, who served as an intermediary between Lord Milner and Zaghloul Pasha, made it clear that the memorandum had no reference to the Sudan, which lay outside the scope of the suggested agreement.

In order to prove how moderate was Zaghloul Pasha's policy, I shall now quote verbatim the analysis given by the *Encyclopædia Britannica* of the Milner-Zaghloul Agreement:

"In order to establish the independence of Egypt on a secure and lasting basis it is necessary to define precisely the relations between Great Britain and Egypt and to modify the privileges and immunities now enjoyed by capitulary Powers. Negotiations between accredited representatives of the Governments should contemplate: a Treaty of Alliance between Great Britain and Egypt under which Great Britain will recognize the independence of Egypt as a constitutional monarchy with representative institutions, and Egypt will confer upon Great Britain the rights necessary to safeguard her special interests and to enable her to give Foreign Powers guarantees which will secure the relinquishment of capitulary rights. Great Britain will defend the integrity of Egyptian territory, *and Egypt will, in case of war, render Great Britain all assistance in her power within her own borders.* This Treaty will stipulate that Egypt will enjoy right of representation in foreign countries, and in absence of an accredited representative confide interests to the British representative; *Egypt will not adopt an attitude inconsistent with the alliance, or enter into any agreement with a foreign Power prejudicial to British interests*; Egypt will confer on Great Britain the right to maintain a military force on Egyptian soil for the protection of her Imperial communications; Egypt will appoint, with concurrence of His Majesty's Government, a financial adviser, who will take over powers now exercised by commissioners of debt, and be generally available for consultation; Egypt will similarly appoint a British official in the Ministry of Justice, with access to Minister, to have cognizance of all matters affecting foreigners and be available for consultation regarding maintenance of law and order; Egypt will recognize the right of Great Britain to intervene in case of legislation operating inequitably against foreigners; the British Representative will have a special position and precedence over other foreign representatives; engagements of British or other foreign officers and officials may be terminated by either party within two years after the Treaty comes into force, with pension or compensation to be therein determined." (*Encycl. Brit.*, Vol. 30, p. 946.)

Further provisions contemplate approval of the Treaty by a Constituent Assembly; validation of all measures taken under martial law; reorganization of mixed tribunals to undertake all jurisdiction hitherto exercised by foreign consular courts; and support of the application of Egypt to be admitted as a member of the League of Nations.

The Milner-Zaghloul Agreement had been well received by the Egyptian public in general and any attempted opposition to the principle of a Treaty of Alliance had met with complete failure. At the same time Zaghloul and his associates, who returned to London in October, 1920, had been urged to support modifications of certain specific points. These contemplated a limitation of the functions of the British Financial Adviser and of the Officer attached to the Ministry of Justice; abandonment of a provision postponing the coming into force of the contemplated Treaty until foreign Powers had agreed to close their consular courts and until agreements had been concluded with the Powers for the abolition of the capitulations; and a formal abolition of the Protectorate.

These reservations, and especially the abolition of the Protectorate, were enthusiastically approved by the whole Egyptian nation when Zaghloul returned to Egypt from France on April 5th, 1921. The Milner Mission, however, adopted the view that no good purpose could be served by further discussion of details at that stage. Zaghloul now opposed the new Egyptian administration formed by Adly Pasha: he declared the Adly Cabinet not to be representative of Egyptian public opinion. The *Encyclopædia Britannica* tells us that at that time moderate opinion in Egypt was unfavourable to Zaghloul's attitude and that he only retained the support of the extremist and the turbulent elements, whose outbreaks in Alexandria and in Cairo on May 20th, 1921, are remembered. Zaghloul issued a manifesto deprecating attacks on foreigners and protested that the riots at Alexandria had nothing to do with politics. In the autumn of 1921 Adly Pasha visited London, where discussions took place between him and the British Government as to the proposed new constitution; but an agreement was not reached, and he returned to Egypt without any further progress having been made.

When the next edition of the *Encyclopædia Britannica* appears it will have to add to its analysis of Egyptian affairs that Zaghloul had the whole Egyptian nation behind him, including the most prominent ex-Prime Ministers, Mohammed Said Pasha and Tewfik Nessim Pasha, who are well known as moderate men, and who are now members of the Zaghloul Cabinet.

It seems to me that it is all-important that England and the British Dominions should be induced to consider the Egyptian point of view, just as it is also only right that Egypt should take into account the British standpoint and the legitimate interests of the Empire.*

Note—In justice to the *Encyclopædia Britannica's* impartial analysis I want to mention that it recognizes the following facts: (1) that the Volunteer Labour Battalions of Egypt played an important part in the conduct of the war; (2) that the requisitions of cereals and of live stock, the control imposed on the price of cotton, the recruiting for the Labour and the Camel Transport Corps, without which the Palestine campaign could not have been brought to a successful conclusion, and, finally, the assumption by the Egyptian Government of the whole liability for expenditure on services connected with the war, held over in a suspense account which reached the amount of three million pounds, constituted a British obligation for which too little credit was given (Vol 30, p. 943). The ever-growing number of British officials tended to absorb administrative functions and not merely to advise. The divulgation of a confidential memorandum regarding the constitution of Egypt and the judicial reforms in favour of English legal procedure and English language in the proposed new courts had roused in 1918 a storm of indignant protest: such facts explain the reservations of Zaghloul with regard to the powers of foreign advisers. The number of British officials increased from 286 in 1896, to 682 in 1906, and to 1,671

XII

Now what are the difficulties to-day, two years after the Declaration of Egypt's Independence, the so-called Declaration of the 28th February, 1922, by virtue of which the Sovereignty of Egypt was recognized by Great Britain on condition that the four reservations contained in that Declaration were first discussed and an equitable solution reached safeguarding the vital interests of the British Commonwealth ?

Let us discuss the secondary difficulties first.

The Declaration of Egypt's Independence demands certain guarantees for the protection of foreign interests, as well as of racial minorities.

in 1919. And they were not always the best type of the English race. The Egyptians objected to their behaviour towards the natives.

But the principal argument I heard against the arbitrary power of British officials was that practically nothing was done for public education in Egypt until the Provincial Councils themselves undertook the reorganization of elementary education. There is a keen demand for education throughout the country. Egyptians protest that during the term of office of Mr. Douglas Dunlop, who was Adviser to the Ministry of Education for thirty years (1889–1919), the problem of Public Education was deliberately neglected. The cost for maintenance of Elementary Schools and Training Colleges for elementary teachers is estimated at over two million pounds a year. Nevertheless, only half a million pounds were granted to Public Instruction in a Budget which covers forty million pounds a year The greatest source of weakness for the decline of all categories of schools was the compulsory introduction of the English language Seventy-six per cent. of the candidates failed. The Provincial Councils maintained 484 elementary schools, attended in 1919 by 30,238 boys and 8,937 girls, while the Ministry of Education maintained only 134 schools attended by 9,521 boys and 8,779 girls.

Zaghloul Pasha and the " Wafd " had already, of their own accord, offered these guarantees in the programme of the National Movement dated the 14th of December, 1918, by suggesting that the *Caisse* of Public Debt should still be kept on with a certain measure of financial control, which was to be discussed in a friendly way. And I know that the continuance of Mixed Tribunals is regarded favourably by the best Egyptian judges, Musulmans as well as Copts, who explained to me that they consider the cordial co-operation of the Mixed Tribunals, between themselves and European judges from various countries, as an excellent institution, as a good school in fact, and that the spirit of international justice which is being thus developed in the practice of the Mixed Tribunals deserves the highest praise. Not only did they applaud the continuance of these Tribunals, but, after the inevitable abolition of the Capitulations, Egypt is anxious to entrust them with jurisdiction over the cases of foreigners, in all such instances as come within the competency of the Tribunals from the point of view of the Penal Code, until such time as with the lapse of years complete confidence between Egypt and the Powers has been established.

As for racial minorities in Egypt, there is but one of importance—the Copts. And they are unanimously in favour of Zaghloul Pasha. From the very beginning, the " Wafd " counted among its members several distinguished Copts who accompanied Zaghloul into exile. The Copts are perfectly contented with the guarantees offered to them by the Egyptian nation, of which they form an integral part; they are a Christian minority of less than a million among over twelve million Musulmans. But the prominent part they have played in the national struggle has endowed them with immense moral prestige. The Cabinet of Zaghloul, if we count Under-Secretaries of State, contains several Copts. Wassif Ghali Pasha, the new Foreign Minister, and Morcos Hanna Pasha, the Minister of Public Works, hitherto President of the Bar, are both Copts. It is impossible for any Foreign Power to be more Coptic than the Copts themselves.

XIII

In order of importance the Reservation (*d*) contained in the Declaration of Independence comes immediately after the clauses upon which I have just touched. It concerns the Sudan.

Two utterly irreconcilable points of view come into conflict over the question of the Sudan. I will first sum up the British position with regard to it.

On the 19th of January, 1899, a Treaty was concluded between England and Egypt by which the two countries together were to carry on the administration of the Sudan. It was known as the Anglo-Egyptian Condominium in the Sudan. In its preamble the Treaty sets forth that after the Sudanese rebellion against the authority of the Khedive, the Sudan having been reconquered "by joint military and financial efforts," the British had acquired "*by right of conquest*" the right of participating in the Administration and Legislation as well as in the development of the Sudan. Among these rights were mentioned *inter alia*:

1. The right of hoisting the British flag on land and sea by the side of the Egyptian flag;

2. Supreme civil and military jurisdiction to be vested in a Governor-General of the Sudan nominated by Egypt, but recommended by the British Government, and removable only with the consent of that Government;

3. This Governor-General to have the power of changing the laws and regulations with regard to the devolution of all property in the Sudan, though notifying any such changes to the British agent in Cairo and the Prime Minister of Egypt.

4. No Egyptian law or decree to be valid in the Sudan except by proclamation on the part of the Governor-General.

5. The jurisdiction of the Mixed Tribunals not to be valid in the Sudan.

6. No Consul, Vice-Consul, or Consular Agent to be nominated without the previous consent of the British Government.

According to the English point of view this Treaty embodies engagements undertaken by Egypt and should be respected in every detail. And public opinion has for a long time been accustomed to regard the Sudan as nothing more nor less than a British possession. In practice, the Treaty of the 19th January, 1899, established the Sovereignty of Great Britain, although it was never actually proclaimed; the Governor General of the Sudan is, to all intents and purposes, the absolute master in his own dominion. A species of mixed Government, both civil and military, was established in the Sudan by Lord Kitchener, and the world has grown accustomed to regarding it as a working proposition in this part of Africa, where, in a territory of over a million square miles, with a population of about four million inhabitants, consisting of Arab and Negroid races, the Englishman has created a business of the first importance in connexion with the cotton industry. A handful of 110 English officials, supported by a few technical experts, carry on the Government of this enormous tract of land. A large number of English capitalists are exploiting the Sudan; important irrigation and drainage works have been, and still are, in process of being carried out, thanks to English initiative. The Sudan to-day constitutes the great hope of Lancashire, and enormous English economic interests are involved in maintaining this sphere of British activity. And that is why Great

Britain refuses even to discuss any revision of the Treaty of January, 19th, 1899 which she regards as *taboo* ; and, calling to witness the sanctity of a signed Treaty, demands recognition of the *status quo*.

The Egyptians, though they recognize that England has developed the Sudan from the economic point of view, maintain that the Treaty of January 19th, 1899, was a purely one-sided arrangement imposed upon the Khedive, but never agreed to by the Egyptian nation. They base this opinion upon their theory of the fundamental illegality of the British occupation ; for where fundamental illegality exists, there is no legal force that can possibly place any moral obligation upon a nation that was never consulted about its destiny between 1882 and 1924. The moment the Khedive became the prisoner of the foreign military authorities in Egypt, his signature ceased to bind the Egyptian people in questions of life and death, such as that of the Sudan. *The right of conquest?* Against the argument of the British right of conquest the Egyptians advance various extremely cogent considerations :

(*a*) After the illegal occupation of 1882, the British military authorities insisted upon the evacuation of the Sudan by the Egyptian troops ; Sherif Pasha, then Egyptian Prime Minister, preferred to resign rather than obey the orders of the Commandant of the British Forces, giving in a famous letter the reason of his resignation as being the fact " that the

British Government says that Egypt must obey its behests *without discussion.*" His successor, Nubar Pasha, an Armenian by race, accepted the English ultimatum and evacuated the Sudan. No Musulman would ever have lent his support to such a step.

(*b*) The Egyptians maintain that the Khedive had no right to sacrifice any portion of Egyptian national territory, of which the Sudan formed an integral part in their eyes. The Firmans incorporated in International Law expressly stipulate that the Sudan was ceded to the Egyptian State, and that the Khedive had no right to surrender any part of it to a foreign power. Lord Salisbury himself declared in 1898 that " the valley of the Nile has belonged and always will belong to Egypt." At the time of the Fashoda incident the British Government insisted upon Colonel Marchand's retreat by asserting that *the Sudan was an Egyptian possession*, and not a territory without a master, (*res nullius*). The Egyptians, who always return to the contention that in the eyes of International Law a territory that was not *res nullius* at the time of a foreign occupation (an occupation which took place in time of peace, without any declaration of war, and entirely based upon an illegal interference in the internal affairs of a properly constituted and recognized State),—and Egypt and the Sudan fall into this category—could not be ceded under pressure from an illegal military force.

(*c*) A third consideration insisted upon by the Egyptians consists in pointing out that the Sudan has cost Egypt between 1896 and 1912 almost eighteen million pounds, not to mention the losses incurred by the fact that owing to this expenditure plans for irrigation and drainage in Egypt itself had to be abandoned. The cotton crop dwindled by at least thirty per cent. in the space of twelve years (1898–1909) and the consequent loss to Egypt has been computed at seventy million pounds. The re-conquest of the Sudan had been accomplished under the direction of England, it is true; but, not to mention the forced evacuation of the Sudan by the Egyptian army owing to an illegal order on the part of the British, the Egyptians had at least spent blood and treasure upon this object. And, as a matter of fact, the garrison in the Sudan consists, according to the report signed by the Sirdar, General Lee Stack, the present Governor General of the Sudan, for the years 1914 to 1919, of 14,000 men composed of Egyptian, black, and Arab regular units. In 1913, Egypt ceased to make any regular contribution to the expenses of the Sudanese administration, but by virtue of a new arrangement she undertook to cede the revenue drawn from the customs on goods coming from, or entering, the Sudan. "It was decided to credit the Sudan with the Customs dues collected in Egypt on goods coming from and going to the Sudan which had previously been collected and retained by Egypt."—"The contribution by Egypt for civil and military expenditure which in 1912 stood at £E.335,000, of which £E.163,000 was on account of the civil expenditure, and £E.172,000 on account of the army, disappeared from the revenue side of the Budget, while the Customs receipts were increased by £E.85,000, this being the figure then estimated as the equivalent of the duties collected in Egypt." (Report of General Lee Stack, 1920, pp. 97-8.) The amount of the previous subvention on behalf of Egypt which started at £E.156,000 in 1899, and rose to £E.268,000 in 1902, had gradually been reduced until it stood at £E.163,000 in 1912. In 1917 Egypt advanced £E.400,000 on certain conditions as to repayment, to prepare and put under cultivation by means of pump irrigation about 19,000 feddans in the Berber and Dongola provinces. (I.C., p. 101.)

(*d*) From the Egyptian point of view there are also two further grievances. In the first place, the Sudanese administration has been blamed for its railway policy. For with Egyptian money it succeeded in diverting commercial activities from the Egyptian ports to Port-Sudan. Long lines of railway were built, intersecting the whole interior of the Sudan, whilst nobody dreamed of connecting Wadi-Halfa with Assouan, which was only 350 kilometres away, doubtless from fear lest the two countries should enjoy easy means of communication with each other.

The Egyptians also insist that the *repartition of the Nile waters between the two countries is unfair.* The construction of the dams in the regions of the Upper Nile, *exposes Egypt to danger if not to death,* an opinion supported by several engineers, including Sir Colin Scott-Moncrieff, who read a paper on the subject at the Royal Institution on the 1st October, 1895. Mr. Tottenham, the present English Under-Secretary of State to the Egyptian Ministry of Public Works, suggested that a Convention should be drawn up by which the Sudan would be forced to supply Egypt, throughout every season of the year, with a certain stipulated quantity of water which should never fall below a given minimum. This quantity was to be determined according to the needs of Egypt and the minimum quantity of water which had originally existed in the Nile. The surplus was to be the property of the Sudan. The question which at once occurred to the Egyptian mind was what the guarantees for this would be, if ever the Sudan, under foreign domination, refused to fulfil her engagements.

In thus summing up the two points of view, and by showing that the Egyptians regard the question of the Sudan as one of life and death for their country, I have merely tried to call attention to the necessity, if any regard is given to fair play, of examining the arguments of the Egyptians and reassuring them as to the intentions of Great Britain. New assurances are of little value if they are not based upon a policy of friendship and mutual trust: properly negotiated treaties are the only sound guarantees.

The Treaty of January 19th, 1899, is not regarded by the Egyptians as a properly negotiated and legally valid treaty, on account of the coercion by which it was extracted. They demand the negotiation of a fresh treaty on all points, for their right, to the Condominium is contained in the text of the contested treaty; and they maintain that they have the right to be consulted and to have their say in safeguarding the vital interests of Egypt towards the Sudan.

Zaghloul Pasha, with whom I have had long and intimate conversations, said to me a few weeks before the elections:

"We are willing to discuss all the questions raised by the problem of Egypt and the Sudan in a spirit of perfect friendliness towards England. We are ready to respect all the legitimate interests of the British as well as of all foreigners. The only point I contest is that those interests should take precedence of the vital interests of Egypt herself. Let us by all means examine *on a basis of equal treatment and legality*, without the intervention of brute force, the arguments on either side. And if we are all animated by good faith, as we are, we shall certainly find a common ground to reconcile the interests of both countries by a duly negotiated Treaty. I say to England: Prove to me that your interests are legally comparable to ours; let us examine together in friendly conversations our respective claims, and let us try to come to an understanding; for this is imperative. But do not have recourse to coercion; if you do, I must retire, for my only weapon is the moral power of Egypt's right. Place your conception of what you consider your interests to be in the balance against our proposals, and I am ready to call upon the conscience of the civilized world to settle the rights and wrongs of the matter."

This is more or less the language always used by Zaghloul throughout 1918 and 1919, as well as during 1921 and 1923. He is prepared to negotiate a treaty of alliance and friendship with England which shall provide all possible moral and legal guarantees to safeguard the supreme interests of both countries.

XIV

But the crux of the whole complicated problem regarding the future relations of England and Egypt lies in the matter of protecting the Suez Canal. The Declaration of February 22nd, 1922, makes direct reference to it in clauses (*a*) and (*b*) reserving "the security of the communications of the British Empire in Egypt; and the defence of Egypt against all foreign aggression or interference, direct or indirect."

The programme of the Egyptian Nationalists demands the neutralization of the Canal, and even the whole of Egypt, under the guarantee of the League of Nations. The neutrality of Egypt, on a similar basis to that of Belgian neutrality, was suggested by Lord Granville in a note of June 16th, 1884, addressed to M. Waddington, then French Ambassador in London. The Egyptians demanded always complete neutrality under the control of an international commission, which should see to it that freedom of navigation in the Suez Canal was preserved, and should prevent any sort of activity menacing the security of communications, as was recommended by the Institute of International Law in 1879. Clauses 1, 2, and 3 of these recommendations call upon the Powers to agree that the freedom of the Suez Canal should be respected by the belligerents in case of war, and, secondly, that neither troops nor munitions of war should be landed except by permission of the territorial power—in this case Egypt—whose neutrality was to be respected *even if Egypt was engaged in war.*

At that time (1879) England did not wish to trust to international engagements but preferred to act on her own account. She raised objections which could not be allowed if ever the League of Nations succeeded in becoming a serious institution. England at that time demanded the admission of vessels of war to the Suez Canal in accordance with a circular from Lord Granville dated the 3rd of January, 1883. The Convention of Constantinople of 1888 remained a dead letter in consequence of the British reservations insisting upon complete liberty of action during the period of British occupation of Egypt. England also insisted upon the possibility of a "sudden emergency," in disregard of the clauses of the Convention of October 29th, 1888, which stipulated that the Canal should not be fortified, and forbade the right of blockading it, to which a French suggestion for making the Canal a neutral zone had been added, but had been rejected by England. The Convention of Constantinople had laid down that the Canal zone should be immune from hostilities three marine miles from its port of entrance, and also from the exercise of all rights of war in these ports. France had suggested that instead of the expression "three marine miles" the following words should be substituted: "No act to prepare directly an operation of war shall be carried out either in the Canal or in its *approaches* or in its ports of access or *in the territorial waters of Egypt*." England refused this definition and preferred to restrict the prohibition to three marine miles, although at that time the range of large guns already exceeded this distance. Russia suggested the neutralization of the Red Sea, which would have meant the neutralization of the Gulf of Aden as well. Again England refused, making the defence of India her excuse, and proclaiming that *the security of the Suez Canal was the supreme law of safety for the British Empire.*

Among the clauses of the Convention of 1888 there are a certain number which might still be of use in future negotiations. For instance: The Powers may not station vessels of war *in* the Canal, but they may do so in the ports of access (Port Said and Suez) limiting the number of vessels to two for each Power. The agents of the Powers in Egypt were to meet together to see that these stipulations were obeyed. They were to meet once a year to insure the execution of the Convention. The Turkish High Commissioner was to preside over these meetings, or, in his absence, a representative of Egypt. Would it not be possible to entrust the Presidency of some similar organization to a representative of Great Britain who, together with an Egyptian representative, would be entrusted with supervising the Suez Canal? The problem obviously consists in securing the observance of any future Convention by means of some proper organization under the ægis of the League of Nations. At one time the Danube Commission was suggested as a model; but England refused this in 1888, and Lord Salisbury preferred a Consular system of supervision. The Consuls' meeting, however, had no right of control over the Egyptian Government. It could only inform that Government that it considered "the

Canal to be in danger," and it was left to the Egyptian Government to protect the Canal against the said danger. The Consuls' meeting could demand the suppression of certain works or of the concentration of troops on one of the banks of the Canal, but they possessed no executive power and their resolutions had to be unanimous. If Egypt had not got at her disposal the means for coping with the danger, she was to appeal to Turkey. Substituting England for Turkey, this clause might still hold good. The Convention of Constantinople is no longer valid, since it rested on the joint guarantees of the Signatory Powers, but its fundamental principles are just and deserve to form the framework of fresh arrangements. One clause above all is important from the Egyptian point of view, namely, *the right of Egypt to defend the Canal with her own forces.* During the negotiations of 1885–9 England had objected to the expression "with her own forces," but in the end she consented to it.

All the clauses, including the Declaration of Disinterestedness, were suspended during the British occupation of Egypt, on account of the general reservations on the part of the British as regards the clauses which, in the opinion of England, interfered with the liberty of action of the British Command. And the Anglo-French Agreement of 1904 did not do much to modify this suspension of the principles of 1888.

XV

My account of the different aspects of the problem shows how the presence of a British army on Egyptian soil complicates the legal solution of all vital questions. Those of my readers who are soldiers will perhaps reply that, on the contrary, it simplifies the problem, and they will argue that as long as Egypt remains a "Military Reservation," for the British Empire, in the strict sense of the word, there is no danger; for soldiers in every age have always preferred a military and strategic safeguard to any legal or moral guarantees. It is in this respect that I find myself in disagreement with the British point of view such as prevailed during the negotiations of 1921. For it is not always necessary to handle the physical forces of a country with a high hand in order efficaciously to defend British interests. The British Commonwealth carries on business fairly well everywhere else in the world, except in the East, whilst contenting itself with Treaties of friendship and commerce, and legal or moral guarantees based upon equality of treatment and reciprocity. Even in the East, things worked much better when, as in the sixteenth and seventeenth centuries, England sought the friendship of the Oriental nations before annexing them. Thus Sir Thomas Roe, the famous Ambassador of Queen Elizabeth, was perfectly successful at the Courts of Soliman the Magnificent and the Grand Moguls of India, whose confidence he succeeded in gaining, with the result that the English nation had a most wonderful trade with the East. In the East more than anywhere else, business means friendship. Hearts must first be won, and trade will follow after. All the Western Powers, with the exception of the United States of America, have tried to dominate the East by brute force, by machine-guns and bayonets, and one can only say that they have failed, in spite of appearances to the contrary which show vast regions of the East as being under the political domination of Europe. *Domination* means and implies *obedience* on the part of those who are dominated. And the East refuses to obey. But it proposes to *negotiate* in the strict etymological meaning of the word: that is to say, to sit on a carpet or about a round table to discuss the terms of some arrangement which would allow everybody to live. For the East desires to live, whilst allowing the West to live, too. Hatred no longer exists in the hearts of the élite of the nations, but merely rapacity, greed of gain, and a hunt after dividends. But all the East demands is its just share, the share which God Himself would refuse to no living creature. Give it that share and your own trade will enter upon a new era of prosperity. For of one thing at least the world is convinced: and that is that, in matters of business, the Englishman is scrupulously faithful to his engagements when once his signature has been placed at the bottom of a contract.

I have spent my whole life in studying the history and psychology of Musulman nations, and I can say with full confidence that the fairest feature of Islamic civilizations consists in the fidelity of the good Musulman to his plighted word. In his history of the international relations of the Ottoman Empire, Hammer-Purgstall gives not a single instance of a Treaty having been broken on the initiative of Moslims. And the personal experience of those who have had to deal with good Musulmans bears testimony to the same fidelity. Where there has been treachery, there has also existed some perversion of sound Islamic traditions. The National movements in Egypt and Turkey have one undoubted characteristic: this consists in the revolt of vital and deep-rooted forces in the Musulman soul against the demoralization of the last centuries, against corruption, and spiritual decadence, by the triumph of a new spirit in the East. This spirit can be expressed in the following words: Self-respect, freedom for self-expression, and the acceptance of Western science as the means of salvation.

I know that the City of London as well as the *Haute Finance* in Paris study only the figures in the Bulletin of the Stock Exchange and that they despise all arguments which cannot be supported by immediate dividends. Nevertheless, I appeal to those among you who realize the value of moral forces, not to refuse to place faith in the tremendous movements that are convulsing the Eastern world. Tempests sometimes break out in the human soul, the purifying power of which becomes visible only long afterwards. It is the fate of man to make mistakes, and to learn his lesson from mistakes. Why should the Eastern nations not receive their political and economic education at their own expense, at the expense, perhaps, of mistakes? For all Western people have made mistakes—and God alone knows how many—before reaching the state of harmony and perfection which we now behold in the hemisphere of the white races. And even in its mistakes the East is copying the West. Why not give it the joy of imitating you, if this gives it any pleasure? When by its mistakes it has learnt that it would be better to preserve the spiritual heritage of its great past, though adapting it to modern science, it will end in finding itself better balanced, healthier and more disposed to listen to its true friends in the West.

But at the present moment the problem of the psychological transformation of the Eastern soul dominates all international affairs, and the great reproach I have to make against European diplomacy as well as British statesmanship is that they have never understood the real issue at stake. They have never understood that you must show confidence in a child which is crying in order to win its confidence; and nations are only big children which are crying because they have lost something.

Who knows whether they will ever find it again? But at least let us help them to look for it . . .

RUSSIA IN ASIA MINOR

THE ORIGINS OF THE ARMENIAN PROBLEM

I

In the great drama of humanity, the final issue of which grows ever more and more beyond the control of those mediocre minds who imagine they hold the wires in their hands, in that colossal tragedy over which the inexorable Fate of the ancients still hovers, Tsarism has without doubt played the most nefarious part. Now that the accredited allies of Russia have recovered the liberty of criticizing the fallen system which for three centuries poisoned the whole atmosphere of Europe, it may perhaps not be out of place to recapitulate a chapter in the foreign policy of the Tsars, the most fundamental bearings of which are far from having been sufficiently understood, in spite of the noisy publicity given to it by certain generous but badly informed minds. The problem to which I refer is that of Armenia, the historical ramifications of which far exceed the numerical importance of the Armenians themselves. The destinies of this little nation, which, until recently, played but a small part in the Eastern question, became suddenly merged in the fate of humanity owing to the intimate ties which bound it to Russia on the eve of the Great War and turned it into the advanced guard of Muscovite policy in Asia Minor. In the preparations for the world drama which we have just witnessed, the Armenian question was amongst those of capital importance which brought the Great Powers to grips, an exceedingly complex question, the undercurrents of which were known only to a few observers well schooled in matters concerning the East. And, during the short interval separating the world war from the *mêlée* in the Balkans, they could not help regarding it with grave anxiety, for they realized the great danger it involved for Europe. If one turns to the parliamentary papers of the House of Commons in 1913, one is at once struck by the presentiments of danger for Europe expressed at that time by several members, whose attention was always fixed upon the Eastern problem, and who time and again asked questions regarding the relations between Russia and Armenia. The respect which the Foreign Office felt obliged to show the Government of the Tsar prevented Sir Edward Grey from devoting the whole of his attention to the danger of which he was warned by such Members of Parliament as Sir Mark Sykes, Walter Guinness, Aubrey Herbert, and others, who were unanimous in declaring that the secret machinations of Russia in Asia Minor were the motive force behind the whole Eastern crisis and were calculated to precipitate a general catastrophe.*

If we listen to the testimony of such men we are forced to conclude that public opinion, led astray by the Press, is apt to draw a sensational but somewhat childish picture of the East, imagining that, as in the fable of the wolf and the lamb, the Musulman is a savage fanatic who spends his life in persecuting the innocent and angelic Christian. In the European myth there is but one guilty party—Islam; and according to it, the Christians in the East are victims without blemish; and Russia, in her capacity of protector of the Orthodox, a fond mother, filled with tenderness for all the oppressed nationalities of Asia. It was thanks to this well-worn myth that the Armenians were able to enjoy the moral protection of the civilized world, and that but few ever tried to find out whether behind the disorders in the East could not be traced the hands of an invisible impresario, working with the object of prolonging the anarchy in these parts, in order to profit by it when the opportune moment arrived. To put all the blame and all the responsibility upon the shoulders

* See the accounts of the proceedings of the House of Commons of the 8th of March and the 1st of July, 1913, and the 17th of March and the 29th of June, 1914, when there were debates on the Armenian question in which Sir Edward Grey, Mr. Acland, the Under-Secretary of State, and Mr. Bryce participated. The fear of Russian intervention was clearly expressed on these occasions and admitted by the representatives of the Foreign Office.

of Islam seemed very convenient to those who are always content with superficial explanations and never give themselves the trouble of probing a question in order to discover the real truth.

But few have ever understood that the poison in the East which paralysed every effort for a renaissance in Islam and an improvement in the relationship between Turks and Christians was identical with the poison with which Tsarism inoculated Russia by separating her morally from Western Europe. For over a century the political physicians of the Ottoman Empire believed that their patient was suffering from an incurable disease, and kept on predicting his speedy demise, without for a moment imagining that the simplest and most efficacious cure would have been to eliminate the poison of foreign intrigue from his system, which in this case was the corrosive acid of the policy of the Tsars. Time and again it was the action of Russia in the East that gave the impulse to all the foreign intrigues in those parts, where the Powers, not wishing to be outdone by the Tsar, combined with him in order to obtain a share of the much coveted "cake." There was a time when this elementary truth was emphasized by one of the most clear-sighted English politicians of the nineteenth century, David Urquhart, and inspired the policy of Great Britain which, under the guidance of Lord Palmerston and Lord Beaconsfield, never ceased to denounce the practices of Russia in the East, without, however, rising to the point of methodically collaborating in the work of raising the Eastern nations themselves. Later on, owing to the exigencies of a European policy which required the friendship of Nicholas II., Great Britain allowed the spiritual direction of the reform movement in the East to drop from her hands, thus breaking a time-honoured tradition and leaving the field clear for the destructive work of Russia. After the Anglo-Russian Entente of 1907, Russia thought the time had come when she might proceed to the realization of her old programme, thanks to the elimination of all resistance on the part of Great Britain—a resistance which had gradually been transformed into strict co-operation with Russia in all matters upon which the destinies of the East depended. And thus the Armenian question became, after the liquidation of Turkey in Europe, the stumbling-block in the path of European policy; and it was thanks to these circumstances that the Armenians suddenly rose to the position of an important factor in the calculations of a diplomacy which, as is always the way, made humanitarian considerations the excuse for masking the most hideous covetousness. The corrosive acid of Tsarism, so magisterially handled by the notorious General Ignatieff, the chemist-in-chief of the policy of destruction in the East, ended by contaminating the whole of international politics. What I should like in the present instance to show in the light of irrefutable evidence, is precisely the subterranean workings of this acid in the case of a particular problem which forms a separate chapter in the diplomatic history of our day.

But let us be perfectly clear about the matter. It is no question of denying or belittling the tragic reality which has made of the Armenian people the most unhappy community in the world. Neither is the value of Armenia to civilization for one moment debated; for no one, as far as I am aware, has ever denied the sterling qualities of her people, which largely contributed to the economic life of the districts they inhabited. As for their morality, which has been criticized by most of the English writers who have had occasion to study it on the spot, I am no believer in the right of one nation to preach morality to others, and I will pass over the chapter dealing with the Armenian character, although, if we may rely on the authority of so eminent an Englishman as Sir Mark Sykes,* the part played by it in the disasters which have overtaken this unfortunate people is by no means despicable. It is not the business of an historian to play the part of preacher; on the contrary, he is better advised to limit his researches to the political, economic, and social causes which together determine a

* Sir Mark Sykes: *The Caliph's Last Heritage*, Macmillan, London, 1915.

problem; for his task is, above all, to know and to understand.

In the Armenian question the network of causes is particularly complex. Instead of repeating hackneyed commonplaces about the fundamental antagonism between Musulmans and Christians, an antagonism which explains nothing, since there are places where these two elements have lived side by side for centuries without waging a war of extermination; instead of lamenting mythical atrocities of which it is impossible to gauge to what extent they were the work of interested conspirators or the hallucinations of an over-heated imagination, the historian must endeavour to unravel the part played by the different factors which together produced what is known as the tragedy of the Armenian race. For tragedy there is; but the question to be examined is whether the parts taken in it have been rightly assigned to those who play the first violin in the concert of the European Press, and whether, from want of precise evidence, the fable of the wolf and the lamb has not been applied somewhat too artlessly to the *tête-à-tête* between the Turk and the Armenian. In the matter of atrocities, Europe set too hideous an example during the years of war to have the right of playing the moralist and the pedagogue to less "civilized" continents. It is a question of assigning to each its place in this tragedy, the general setting of which bears all too close a resemblance to the time-honoured methods of the Tsarist system, the methods of Peter the Great in the Ukraine, of Catherine II. in the extermination of Poland, of Alexander I. in Greece, and of Nicholas I. and his successors in the Balkans and in Asia, to allow of any doubt in the minds of those who know the true motive power behind the Eastern question. The fact that Tsarism may occasionally have contributed indirectly to the welfare of the peoples into whom it dug its claws, although it desired evil for evil's sake, cannot change duly-established historical truths which prove it to have been the most malignant force of modern times.

In order to understand the true significance of the Armenian problem on the eve of the World War, we must, before proceeding any further, define the terms in which the Turkish question was presented to Europe. In his *Letters from Turkey*, dated 1835 to 1836, Marshal Moltke, then a Captain attached to the Ottoman army, and one of the most acute observers of the Near East, points out with some surprise that Europe took more interest in Turkey than the Turks themselves. If this remark was not strictly in accordance with the truth even in the time of Sultan Mahmoud II., who made serious efforts to win over the Turks to his new ideas, it is in no way applicable to the Turkey of the present day, where the most humble "hamal" takes as passionate an interest in public affairs as any politician.

Moltke compares the reforms attempted by Mahmoud II. to those which Peter the Great successfully carried out in Russia, and observes that the continual intervention of the European Powers at Stamboul did perhaps more to hinder all serious reform than the antiquated spirit of the Turks at the beginning of the nineteenth century. The complete isolation enjoyed by Russia under Peter the Great allowed the latter to work protected from the curiosity of Europe, and to apply the strong hand without fear that external intrigues would exploit the discontent inevitably aroused by reformers always and everywhere ; whilst Turkey was obliged constantly to fight not only against the reactionary spirit of the "Old Turks," but, above all, against the intrigues of foreign Powers.

Without drawing the conclusion that must be obvious to any impartial observer, Moltke here touched upon the primordial cause which has for a century retarded the renaissance of Islam. The multifarious requirements of Europe which were guided by no knowledge of the Oriental spirit, were among the principal obstacles to the movement for reform in Turkey, which wore itself out in an unequal struggle to ward off the stranglehold of Europe from the last vestiges of Ottoman sovereignty. In this prolonged struggle it would have been possible for the Turkish reformers long ago to have succeeded by means of their own efforts, without copying

Peter the Great, whose ferocity and violence are well known. All Orientalists of standing, in England as well as elsewhere, are agreed that the Koran nowhere forbids the reorganization of the political institutions of Islam, the essentially democratic spirit of which lends itself to the most modern reforms, provided they adopt a Musulman shape, and are initiated by an independent Mohammedan government, free from all external pressure. The character of the Anatolian peasant, which has been extolled to the skies by every Englishman who came into contact with him during the War, does not require the brutal methods which other nations have had to undergo before entering upon the path of reform; his traditional habit of obedience affords ground for the belief that he would without resistance accept the most radical changes, provided he were instructed in that branch of knowledge in which he is most ignorant—that is to say, given some elementary notions on the science of agriculture, upon which his prosperity depends.

If I am emphasizing this point before proceeding with my subject, it is because the Armenian question has always been represented in Europe as a traditional conflict between "Musulman fanaticism," always hostile to the civilization, and the spirit of Armenia, which, ever since there have been Armenians in Asia Minor, has always endeavoured to approach the West. But this antagonism is nothing but the artificial product of foreign intrigues, and a fairly recent product to boot; for a mere glance at the history of Turco-Armenian relations in the past proves that the two races lived on good terms with each other for several centuries without a conflict of any magnitude supervening to separate them. The fact that must strike all observers who have made anything approaching a profound study of Ottoman history, is that all the racial conflicts within the Empire were the creation of the foreigner, without whose interference the various nationalities would have lived side by side in peace, and carried out all necessary reforms by common consent. At all events the agreements reached between Mohammed the Conqueror and the nations which Byzantium left as a legacy to the newly-formed Turkish Empire, prove the truth of this hypothesis; these agreements were not brutally "imposed," as is generally believed, but were the result of prolonged negotiations between the Turks and the conquered peoples—peoples who did not expect to be treated as nation to nation by the victors who put an end to the Byzantine Empire. Only too little is known of this chapter in history, which gives a better idea of the true character of the Turks than all the accounts of modern European globe-trotters. People are apt to forget that the Turks were greeted as liberators from the yoke with which the Byzantine clergy had oppressed the people, that Mohammed the Conqueror allowed the Christians freedom of conscience, which until then had been a thing unknown in the whole of Europe, and that Islamic tolerance preceded Western tolerance by over two centuries. I would only ask you to read the admirable work which a well-known English thinker, Professor Sir Thomas W. Arnold, published in 1896, and of which a second edition appeared in 1913, in the very midst of a Turcophobe crisis in Europe. It is entitled *The Preaching of Islam: A History of the Propagation of the Moslim Faith.* It shows that the object of the Musulman armies has never been to force conversion upon the Christians. It was a question of ruling, but not of converting them. The Christians of Asia Minor were delighted to find themselves delivered from the tyranny of the Byzantine clergy. The more recent researches of a great Italian Orientalist, Don Leone Caetani, Prince of Teano and Duke of Germonetta, confirm the thesis of the English professor. In the *Annals of Islam,* written with great skill, Don Leone Caetani has raised a monument to Mohammedan tolerance, which is without parallel, in spite of the despotic governments which later disfigured Islam. The fact that the Turks inaugurated a specifically feudal system with regard to the Christians by reserving to themselves the reins of government in the state, was not an abnormal proceeding at the time of the conquest; the fate of the subject peoples was in no way comparable with the fate of the races ruled by the harsh feudal system that was established in Christendom until the French Revolution. Moreover, it is impossible to make comparisons between the Musulman East and modern Europe, for it must never be forgotten that Islam is only fourteen hundred years old, and a difference of six hundred years from the social point of view precludes any premature verdict regarding the progress of which Musulman society is capable.

The Armenians were one of those Christian nations who in the past owed to Turkey the maintenance of their religion and their culture. They were already a conquered people when Mohammed delivered them from the domination of Byzantium. The periods during which they existed as independent states were extremely short, and they were enfeoffed to all the conquerors who appeared in Asia Minor. Owing to their great and incontestable qualities, they played a very important part in the Byzantine Empire, when their barons filled the highest offices in the administration and in the diplomatic service. And this part they were able to preserve intact under Turkish rule so long as they remained loyal to Turkey. When Mohammed entered Constantinople, he summoned Ovakim, the Armenian Bishop of Broussa, and receiving him with the highest honours, established him in Constantinople, appointed him Patriarch of all the Armenians, and conferred upon him political and religious privileges which secured the liberties of his people in the new Empire. Moreover, the Armenian barons hastened to offer their services to the Sultan, as they had always done whenever a new conqueror appeared in their country. And until quite recently they were able to maintain the important position which they had won in the Government, the Sublime Porte being always open to their administrative and diplomatic talents, and the Turks for long regarding them as constituting the only Christian element whose loyalty was proof against the Muscovite ambitions which threatened both alike. In ancient documents the Armenians are described as *milleti sadika* (the faithful people) in recognition of the great devotion they had shown to the State. During the nineteenth century it was regarded as an article of faith by clear-sighted Armenians to prefer Turkish to Russian rule, provided that, under the ægis of Turkey, they were given full freedom for the development of their national culture, their language and their religion. The radical change which has taken place in this respect since the Congress of Berlin in certain Armenian centres is undeniable, but the explanation is not to be sought in Hamidian massacres, or Kurdish brigandage. We shall see why.

Many centuries of Turco-Armenian collaboration, weighed against thirty or forty years of racial conflict, should make every historian who is anxious to make a profound study of his subject pause and reflect instead of being content with the hackneyed explanations of events in the East given in the daily Press. The Armenian question had not yet entered into the domain of diplomacy when other races belonging to the Ottoman Empire had already been snatched away by Russia. During the War of Greek Independence, the Armenian Church was entirely absorbed by internal disputes, and the Sublime Porte was obliged to protect the Armenian sects which the Patriarchate wished to persecute. If Armenian Protestants have not always enjoyed liberty of conscience, it is because the Patriarchs themselves gave the signal for persecution. It required the intervention of the Sublime Porte to prevent various sects of Christians from flying at each other's throats, just as it required the protection of the Musulman police to prevent Orthodox and Catholic monks in Jerusalem from murdering each other in front of the sacred places. Armenian writers were for long almost unanimous in agreeing that their co-religionists enjoyed far greater liberty in Turkey than in Russia, and it is only since the melancholy rule of Abdul Hamid, which enjoyed the protection of certain great Powers, in spite of its degenerate character, that the gulf dividing Turks and Armenians was fixed.*

* The responsibility for the massacres of Adana in 1909 has been imputed to the new régime. The report issued by Agop Effendi Babikian, the Armenian Deputy for Rodosto, who was entrusted with the task of enquiring into the massacres, did indeed establish the guilt of the local officials and certain members of the local committee of Adana ; but it is asserted that among

The new régime made some attempts to remedy this, but the evil was too deeply rooted to be destroyed in a day. The world war laid bare the abyss to its depths and gave the Armenian question its true significance.

II

The complexity of the Armenian problem lies in the fact that it presents various aspects according to the periods studied and the standpoint adopted. There was a time when the Armenians were the *bête noire* of Russia, and when Turkey was their one refuge against the policy of extermination pursued against them by the Russian governors of the Caucasus. At another period Nicholas II. and Abdul Hamid outrivalled each other in brutality in the Armenian districts submitted to their authority. Everyone knows that in 1895 and 1896 it was the attitude of the Tsar and his counsellors that encouraged the "Red Sultan" in his horrible policy at the time of the Armenian massacres. It was then that Prince Lobanoff-Rostowski, the Russian Minister for Foreign

those who rallied to the new régime directly after the revolution there were to be found many reactionaries in disguise, who joined the Committee of Union and Progress with the object of compromising it at the first opportunity. The Committee of Adana was composed of such people, and it required time for the new régime to rid itself of these dangerous elements. Their punishment by the Porte proves the hollowness of the accusation.

Affairs, gave the *mot d'ordre* that for Russia it was preferable to have on her frontiers an "Armenia without Armenians," since the Armenian merely presented an obstacle to Russian designs, and that without him it would be easier for Russia to absorb the so-called Armenian provinces when the day arrived for the partition of Asia Minor. Twenty years later the Revolutionary Federation of Armenia preached hatred of both Abdul Hamid and Nicholas II., including in its European propaganda a crusade against the two autocrats whom a similar fate overtook at an interval of ten years. Could any more formidable indictment be brought against a system of oppression than the twenty-four letters written by the Armenian author Aknouni, a French translation of which was published at Geneva in 1905 by the Revolutionary Federation of Armenia, under the ægis of Francis de Pressensé !* Here it is clearly shown how mistaken were the Armenians, who, during the nineteenth century, allowed themselves to be seduced by the promises of the Tsars. From the day when the first corps of Armenian volunteers made its appearance in the Russian Army at the time of the war of 1826, in order to help the Tsar to seize Etchmiadzine, the ancient sanctuary of Orthodox Armenians, from the occasion of the first visit in 1837 of Nicholas I. to the "heart" of the province of Ararat, to which he had promised independence,

* E. Aknouni, *Les Plaies du Caucase*, Geneva, 1905.

to the promises made in 1878 and 1913, the Armenians had a thousand opportunities to convince them that Russia was knowingly deceiving them, and abusing their national sentiments and their natural inclination towards Slav Orthodoxy.

The idea of a "Kingdom of Ararat" never ceased to haunt the minds of the Armenian revolutionaries from the time that Catherine II. issued her appeal to the peoples of the Caucasus and the first programme of Armenian independence was drawn up and submitted for the approbation of the Tsarina by Archbishop Joseph Arghoutian. The first negotiations between the Armenians and the Russian Government resulted in the eighteenth century in the following provisos:

1. That the Armenian provinces shall form a separate kingdom under the protection of Russia. 2. That the Armenians shall pay a tax to Russia and furnish her with troops in case of war. 3. That the country shall be governed by its own laws. 4. That a certain number of Russian troops shall remain in the Armenian provinces for a given period for the protection of the inhabitants and to guard the country. 5. The right of appointing the King of Armenia to be vested in the Empress of Russia. 6. The capital to be Erivan or Vagharchabat. The flag of Armenia to be a tricolour. 7. The two countries to sign a treaty of commerce and a fiscal agreement.

In vain did the Armenians await the realization of these promises. The Tsars overwhelmed them with flattering words whenever they had need of

Armenian volunteers, but when it was a question of translating promises into action, they turned a deaf ear. The way in which the Catholicos Nerses of Aschtarak was deceived is well known. He put himself at the head of the Armenians who volunteered against Persia and the only reward he received was a decree of thanks from Nicholas I. In order to rid themselves of the embarrassing demands of this old man, the Russian Government did not hesitate to have recourse to violence, and when Nerses died unexpectedly in 1857, public opinion was convinced that the Russian Government had had him poisoned in order to send the programme of Armenian independence to the grave with him.* The same deceptive fate awaited the Armenian movement which Grigor Artzrouni, a publicist, inaugurated in December, 1876, in expectation of the Russo-Turkish War, which broke out two years later. A manifesto addressed to Alexander II. invited the Tsar to come to the help of "a brother nation" beyond the Caucasus.† In this manifesto, which was placed in the hands of the Grand Duke Michael Nicolaïevitch, in the palace of Tiflis, by a Russo-Armenian deputation, the following passage may be found:

"Knowing the sympathy which our well-beloved King and the whole of Russia feel for the fate of the

* Aknouni, *Les Plaies du Caucase*, p. 210.
† Aknouni, *op. cit.*, p. 212.

Christian subjects of Turkey, we, their brethren by blood and religion, place all our hope for the amelioration of their condition in the power of Russia, and we put our entire confidence in the all-powerful Emperor."

The only result of all this trouble on their part was Article 16 of the Treaty of San Stefano, which promised the Turkish Armenians "such improvements and reforms as local conditions necessitated," an article which, with a few formal modifications, was inserted in the statute drawn up by the Congress of Berlin (Article 16), and which roused the first suspicions in the Moslim world regarding the secret intentions of certain parties in Armenia. Without being of any practical use to the Armenians themselves, this article played a capital part in the various interventions which the Powers regarded it as necessary to make in Turkey after the Congress of Berlin, in order to deprive Russia of the privilege of "protecting" the Christians. England armed herself with a similar weapon by the Convention of Cyprus, which gave her direct influence in the Armenian question. Before passing to the study of the melancholy consequences which this constant intervention entailed for the Turkish Armenians, whose lot until then had been supportable, let me say a few words about their social and political condition in the middle of the nineteenth century.

During this period, between the Crimean War and the Russo-Turkish War of 1878, the Armenian question was of small interest to Europe. The Turks were still the pampered children of English Conservatives, and Asia Minor was *noli me tangere* to the whole of Western diplomacy. The political literature of England and France was constantly trying to prove that the Turks were an infinitely more sympathetic race from the point of view of Western civilization than were the Russians, whose dangerous ambitions Monsieur de Massade repeatedly denounced. His articles published in the *Revue des Deux Mondes* during the Crimean War prove how easy it is for a journalist, inured to polemics, to find arguments in favour of any cause ; for what strikes the reader of these old chronicles by a French academician is the fact that he fought Tsarism with the same weapons which are to-day being used against Turkey in the name of civilization. At that time those who knew Islam hastened to prove by precepts drawn from the Koran how humane and gentle was that religion, and how far superior to Russian Orthodoxy, that Orthodoxy which the Church of England is now beginning to find full of admirable qualities, since the political exigencies of the moment have associated Great Britain with the destructive policy of the Tsars in the East.* But

* On the subject of the *rapprochement* between the Orthodox Church and the Church of England (the High Church Party) see the Russian Supplement of *The Times* of the 25th of March, the 24th of June, and the 29th of July, 1916. See also "Intercommunication Between the Church of England and the Orthodox

more deserving of attention than the Russophobe Press of the countries which at that time were combating the ambitions of Tsarism in the East, is the voice of the Armenians in Turkey. The latter were far from identifying themselves with the agitation of their kinsmen in the Caucasus, who wished to "confide their fate entirely into the hands of the all-powerful Tsar." On the contrary, their most highly accredited representatives seized every possible occasion for condemning this agitation in the European Press, by pointing to the progress made by Turkish Armenians, progress that had been realized by legal methods within the Ottoman Empire. Again in 1867, Prince Dadian, an Armenian of high repute, rendered homage to Ottoman rule in an important article published in the *Revue des Deux Mondes.* This exceedingly interesting description of Armenian society in the first half of the nineteenth century brought forward evidence to show how the Armenians of Turkey might proceed in perfect freedom to the democratization of their ecclesiastical institutions, without their social development being in any way hampered by the Turks.*

In this article Prince Megherditch Dadian depicts the progress made by the Armenians after the promulgation of the Tanzimat, the charta which gave

Church of Russia" in *Le Correspondant* of the 25th of August, 1916, pp. 708–32.

* *La Société Arménienne Contemporaine, Revue des Deux Mondes*, June, 1867, pp. 903–28.

the political franchise to the Christian communities in Turkey. The Patriarch of Constantinople was, as we know, not only the spiritual but also the temporal chief of his people, and their official intermediary with the Government. Nevertheless, his religious power, like that of all the archbishops and bishops of the Armenian Church, was derived until the late War from the Catholicos of Etchmiadzine, the supreme head of the whole of Armenian Orthodoxy.* As long as the Catholicos maintained his independence with regard to the Tsars, no grave disturbance troubled the political relations of Turks and Armenians. Until the promulgation of the ecclesiastical constitution of the Armenians in 1860, the power exercised by the Patriarch over his clergy was of an autocratic nature that almost amounted to omnipotence. The Sublime Porte interfered in nothing, but contented itself with collecting the *kharadj* (the poll tax), the payment of which was made under the guarantee of the Patriarch, and through his agents. The combined civil and religious power of the Patriarchate might have exercised a beneficent influence even at the time when the Christians were not on an equal footing with the Musulmans, had it not been seized by an Armenian oligarchy consisting of parvenus who had made their fortunes in banking and commerce and appropriated the Patriarchate

* The celebrated monastery situated at the foot of Mount Ararat and founded at the beginning of the fourth century by the Armenian Apostle, Saint Gregory, surnamed the Illuminator.

to their own advantage. The National Council created by this faction was, according to Dadian, merely a permanent centre of intrigue and discord in the hands of whose members the Patriarch was a docile instrument. The masses in Armenia, organized into industrial guilds (*esnaf*) played no part in affairs. They were quite powerless in the face of every kind of abuse on the part of their own rulers, and their grievances were consistently shelved by the supreme council of the Armenian Church. At length the guilds implored the mediation of the Sultan, which resulted in 1844 in the reorganization of the supreme council into which were admitted fourteen members, chosen by the Patriarch from the industrial guilds. In 1847, two councils were formed to sit with the Patriarch, the first an ecclesiastical council to exercise surveyance over his actions in the spiritual domain, and the second a lay council consisting of twenty members, elected by the guilds, to take charge of civil affairs. The Patriarch was President of both councils, but he ceased to play the part of the lawful intermediary between his people and the Sublime Porte. His functions were confined to those of a *logothetes*, or chancellor, charged with the execution of the decisions of the civil council. By a firman of the Sultan of the 6th of March, 1847, approving of these changes, the democratization of the Armenian Church made a great advance. The Armenian people won the right of appointing their own chiefs and their own representatives. Thirteen years later, on the 24th of May, 1860, it extracted a constitution from its rulers, which placed its internal administration upon a democratic basis. Universal suffrage was the rule at all elections; the powers of the Patriarch were subordinated to the control of the general assembly, by which he was elected. Two councils, called national councils, the one religious and the other civil, offshoots of the general assembly, took charge of the management of ordinary affairs. Administrative, judicial, educational, and financial committees were entrusted with the economic supervision of the various foundations and national concerns, regulated the courts, inspected the schools, etc. This constitution has been modified on various occasions since its promulgation down to the time of its most recent revision by the Government of the Young Turks (August, 1916); but its fundamental principle is that the Armenians should form within the Ottoman Empire a separate nation which, during the whole of the nineteenth century, had no reason for envying the Armenians of Russia. The Armenian Press had undergone considerable development since its first organ, the *Aurora*, was founded in 1839 at Smyrna, and Prince Dadian maintains that it was never shackled in any way in Turkey nor subjected to any foreign pressure. Anybody at that time could found a journal without leave having been previously obtained or security given, and everybody enjoyed full liberty for the expression of opinion. Later on the Porte laid down certain restrictions, taking as model the regulations which obtained with the French Press in the middle of the nineteenth century, but which in no way hindered the discussion of any question of general interest.* But with the growth of Armenian separatism in the Ottoman Empire these liberties were further restricted, until in the end they were abolished altogether.

The reign of Abdul Hamid intervened which made Turkey uninhabitable for every race within its borders, Musulmans and Christians alike. But at least it did not touch the fundamental privileges which the Armenians had won from previous Sultans, which allowed them to organize themselves within their own borders and to live their own life, until the time when the massacres, which took place in the last decade of the nineteenth century, revealed the true issues of the Armenian question to Europe. This question was created in all its magnitude by the foreign intervention which rendered no real service to the Armenians, but merely roused the Turks in opposition to new pretensions which were in their eyes incompatible with the existence of their country. Except for the reign of Abdul Hamid, Turks and Armenians got on far better together during their

* Dadian, Amora, pp. 908–15, 924.

tête-à-tête of six hundred years than Russians and Armenians had done during the rule of the Tsars in the Caucasus, and nothing can on principle justify the assertion that after the fall of Abdul Hamid it was impossible to reopen the question and secure co-operation between Turks and Armenians for the benefit of the districts inhabited by both races. Unfortunately for their own cause, many Armenians turned ever more and more towards Russia, who, pretending to have been converted to the idea of an autonomous Armenia, deluded them by promises of a material prosperity to be secured under the ægis of the Tsars.

If we compare the situation of the Armenians in the Caucasus with that of their Ottoman brethren down to the end of the nineteenth century, we shall find in the first case that material prosperity had been won owing to the capacity of the Armenians for utilizing the great Russian markets in order to develop their trade, whilst the Armenians in Asia Minor suffered, as did also the Turks and every other element in the Ottoman Empire, from the absolute stagnation to which Abdul Hamid condemned his unfortunate country for over thirty years. But, from the political point of view, Russia was until quite recently, far from giving her Armenian subjects a tenth of the liberty enjoyed by their brothers in Turkey since the Ottoman conquest. I have already mentioned the deception practised by the Tsars upon the first battalions of Armenian volunteers who ranged themselves on the side of the Russian army in all the wars which the latter fought during the nineteenth century. But for a few purely formal concessions which were calculated to stir the popular imagination, such as the blessing of the Armenian standard in the cathedral of Tiflis and the grandiloquent manifestos addressed to the Armenians by the Commanders-in-Chief of the Russian army on the opening of a campaign in which Armenian volunteers were to play a part, nothing of any account has ever been done by Russia for the benefit of a people whose simplicity she has always exploited in order to humble them without mercy when she no longer had need of their blood. The closing of the Armenian schools in 1885, the confiscation of ecclesiastical property to the value of a hundred millions, in spite of the recognition by the Russian Government in 1836 of the right to property vested in the Gregorian-Armenian Church; the arrest of the intellectual *élite* of the Caucasus; the monstrous action brought against the Dachnakzoutioun party (the revolutionary Federation of Armenia founded in 1890); every kind of Russianizing measure, administrative crimes, banishment, deportation, rabid war upon the Armenian language, confiscation of public and private property—such was the political condition of the Armenians in Russia until the beginning of the twentieth century. Even as late as 1905, it was illegal to give a lecture in Armenian in Tiflis, an Armenian centre, or in any other town in the Caucasus.* And the most intimate colleague of Abdul Hamid in the task of suppressing the Armenians was that same Prince Lobanoff-Rostowski who directed the foreign policy of the Tsar during the most tragic moments in the history of this "kindred nation."

Directly after the Russo-Japanese War the picture changes. For to Russia, beaten in the Far East and already a prey to revolution, some pretext was required for "returning to Europe," as the diplomatic expression has it—that is to say, for returning to her ancient practices with regard to the Eastern question and for imposing herself upon Europe as the liberator of the Christians of Asia Minor, since, in Europe itself there were no Christians left to be "liberated," except those whom Tsarism still held in its grip. It was then that the authorities in St. Petersburg realized that the methods hitherto employed in the Caucasus, which had ended in provoking an international scandal, were not calculated to secure the sympathies of the Armenians in Turkey. On the advice of Count Vorontzoff-Dachkoff, the Lieutenant-General of the Tsar in the Caucasus, and the intimate friend of Nicholas I., the Russian Government reversed the machine, returned the property that had been confiscated

* See Aknouni, *Les Plaies du Caucase*, p. 223.

from the Armenian Church, reopened the schools, and put an end to political lawsuits and various grievances, in order to conciliate the Armenians and win them over to the cause of Russia in Asia Minor. It was a matter of stopping the separatist agitation among the Armenians of the Caucasus by dazzling their eyes with visions of their old programme of a kingdom of Ararat, enlarged into a kingdom of Armenia by the annexation of a large portion of Asia Minor under the sceptre of the Tsar, whose title of " Tsar of the Armenian nations " was invoked —a title which figures among the innumerable denominations of the Emperors of all the Russias. Vorontzoff-Dachkoff, supported by Armenian advisers, set to work with great skill, and in a few years succeeded in setting in motion the entire machinery of a subterranean policy in Asia Minor, the importance of which did not become evident until the World War gave Russia the opportunity of reaping the fruits of this patiently elaborated manœuvre. In 1913, in a report sent to Nicholas II., Count Vorontzoff-Dachkoff states with satisfaction that the Armenians were becoming ever more and more attached to the Russian Government,* and at the same time the *Novoïa Vremia* exclaimed : " What a change of ideas and sentiments ! The leaders of Armenian society have returned to the bosom of

* Maxime Kovalevsky, *La Russie et la Question Arménienne*, *La Revue Politique Internationale*, April, 1914.

Russia, their mother." In the Duma, Papadjanoff, a Russian Armenian, and a member for Transcaucasia, demanded that Russia should take in hand the "realization" of reforms in the Turkish Empire, and Milioukoff cited the Treaty of San Stefano, which placed the whole of the Upper Euphrates within the frontiers of Russia.* No mention was made of the Armenian pogroms of 1905 in the towns of Bakou, Choucha, Minkend, etc., massacres organized by the *agents provocateurs* of the Tsar, when, according to the testimony of Russian Socialist writers, whole families had been wiped out, including children of tender years.† Formerly the Musulmans of the Caucasus had been incited against the Armenians; now the latter were to be used as weapons in the struggle against Turkey. Unfortunately for the Armenians, they allowed themselves to be inveigled into the trap.

Russia, in this matter, was in a strong position owing to the fact that the chief heads of the Armenian Church were entirely subject to the Russian Court. The Catholicos of Etchmiadzine, who had formerly been independent, had become a mere creature of the Tsar, to whom he had to swear an oath of fealty. During the course of the nineteenth century, after the religious centre of Armenia had fallen into the power of Russia, the Government of the Tsar spared

* Michel Pavlovitch, *La Russie et les Arméniens* (*La Revue Politique Internationale*. May, 1914. pp. 464–5.)

† *Ibid.*, p. 467.

no effort to place in the pontifical seat only such prelates as were well disposed towards Russia. In order to win the sympathy of the Armenians and prepare the way for Russian domination over their compatriots in Asia Minor, the support of the Catholicos of Etchmiadzine was exceedingly useful, and it was necessary to increase his prestige outside his own country, whilst at home using all the means, both violent and gentle, at the disposal of the Tsar, to keep him in a state of subjection. Every effort on the part of Constantinople in a contrary direction proved vain. More than once the Porte endeavoured to secure the supremacy of the Catholicos of Cis and Aghtamar, especially of the former of these towns, the geographical position of which (in Cilicia) placed it within the sphere of Muscovite influence. In this way Turkey hoped to weaken the prestige of Etchmiadzine and raise a wall between Turkish Armenians and the pontifical seat of Ararat.* Until the Great War, which gave Turkey the opportunity of decreeing the complete separation of the Patriarchate of Koum-Kapou from the Catholicos of Etchmiadzine, the influence of the latter remained unimpaired; and all the bishops of the Gregorian Church of Armenia had to receive the sacrament from him. It can easily be imagined what this meant in the way of political influence in countries where political life was intimately bound up with religious

* Aknouni, *Les Plaies du Caucase*, p. 121.

life. The close connexion between the Catholicos of Etchmiadzine and the Tsar, and the supreme power exercised by the latter over the Armenian episcopacy in Turkey, allowed Russia to place at the head of the Turkish Armenians only such prelates as were devoted to her cause, who were merely so many agents of the Tsar, and obliged to swear oaths of fealty to "the Tsar of the Armenians' before they could be consecrated bishops by the Catholicos.*

The latter could not get into touch with the Armenians inhabiting Europe except through the medium of the Russian Foreign Minister. Any documents, letters, and bulls which were communicated to Europe in a roundabout way without the intervention of this Minister, were regarded as proofs of disloyalty to the Government.† Until 1885 the election of the Catholicos was conducted in such a way as to allow the successful candidate the minimum of independence. Nerses Varjapetian who was elected in 1884, and who, as Patriarch of Constantinople, had taken a share in the drafting of Article 61 of the Congress

* In the month of August, 1916, the new organic statute of the Armenian Patriarchate was passed, forbidding all communication between the Armenian Church in Turkey and the Catholicos of Etchmiadzine. The Catholicos of Cis and Aghtamar were re-united with the Patriarchate of Constantinople and of Jerusalem. The Catholicos of the Sacred City, whose seat was the Convent of Saint Jacob Marjacob, was given the entire jurisdiction over Turkish Armenians. The statute of 1916 provided for new regulations for the election of the Patriarch and the ecclesiastical councils, as well as for the reorganization of the administrative councils of the Patriarchs and the Bishops.

† Aknouni, *Les Plaies du Caucase*, p. 122.

of Berlin, was, it is true, still able to impose conditions upon the Russian Government before accepting the episcopate. But his proposals were disregarded and in the following year Russia ordered a fresh election to be held, in which she brought pressure to bear and secured the choice of her own candidate, who was a docile instrument in the hands of the Tsar. The consent of the Tsar was necessary for the nomination of the Catholicos, and all freedom in the election was destroyed by the very fact that the candidate who wished to secure the imperial sanction was obliged to undertake to support the policy of Russia, without which no Catholicos stood a chance of being accepted by St. Petersburg. The Patriarch of Constantinople, who received his investiture from the Sultan, was in a very different position as regards political freedom, for until quite recently he was able to share in any action directed against the authority of the Sublime Porte. The Catholicos could not even appoint the bishops he wished, or members of the Synod ; even his right to ordain what priests he liked was restricted, not to mention the fact that he was surrounded by the spies of the Russian Government.*

When it was a matter of using the authority of the Catholicos in order to intimidate the Armenians, the Russian Government supported him, whilst in Turkey it was thanks to the active assistance of the

* Aknouni, *Les Plaies du Caucase*, p. 137.

Government that the democratization of the ecclesiastical institutions of the Armenians was accomplished at so early a date.*

The Catholicos, thus tied to the apron strings of Russia, proved an exceedingly useful instrument on the eve of the War, when it was a question of mobilizing public opinion in Europe in favour of Russian intervention in the Armenian problem. The Catholicos was introduced as the supreme head of the whole nation begging the help of the Tsar on behalf of his persecuted flock. In the summer of 1912, on the eve of the Balkan War, he was summoned to St. Petersburg, the moment being judged opportune for raising the question of Asia Minor before Europe, as well as all the other problems connected with the Ottoman Empire. Shortly after the mission of Daneff to Livadia, when the Tsar gave his sanction to the Balkan conventions directed against Turkey in Europe, the Catholicos appeared in solemn audience before Nicholas II., in order to have conferred upon him the highest Russian decoration, as well as to receive definite instructions from the Tsar with regard to a great combined Russo-Armenian policy which was to complete the Balkan policy, and of which the frankly avowed object was to liquidate the whole of the Eastern question to the benefit of pan-Slavism.†

* Dadian, *Aurora*.

† René Pinon, in the *Bulletin du Comité de L'Asie Française*, 1913, p. 294.

III

Before studying in detail the setting of this great Russo-Armenian plan, which was a perfect model of subterranean diplomacy, magisterially prepared and executed both as regards its avowed aims and also as regards those objects which diplomacy never reveals, a few pages must be devoted to the social aspects of Turco-Armenian relations.

Apart from its diplomatic bearings, the Turco-Armenian problem was *par excellence* a social and agrarian problem. In a country which had been neglected for centuries under a bad economic system, and inhabited by a mixture of primitive races, it was a question of creating a new life capable of embracing the diverse elements which had mingled and struggled together since the great migrations poured into Asia Minor the surplus populations of every race and every religion. There where Europe and Asia meet without coalescing, and without even understanding each other, the task of a modern State should have been to secure the orderly cohabitation of all these diverse elements, to unite them in one whole, and to draw from the soil, the richness of which was once proverbial, all the moral and material riches lying dormant beneath it. Instead of fulfilling this task, the Ottoman conquerors merely superimposed themselves upon a condition of affairs already in existence at the time of their appearance, contenting themselves with deriving the greatest possible benefit from the subject races, whilst leaving their institutions and liberties untouched. In assuming the position of a conquering race, the Turks had the good sense not to place any obstacle in the way of the internal development of the countries they had inherited from the Byzantine Empire and who submitted without much difficulty to their new masters. The understanding reached between the conquerors and the subject races bore the brand of political inequality, it is true, but the contempt affected by the Musulmans for the conquered in no way prevented the latter from playing their economic and social part within the confines of the Empire. And this contempt became in reality a source of weakness for the Turks, who ended by realizing that while they had rested on their laurels the rest of the world had advanced. When they awoke it was too late. The Christians of the East had already drawn too close to Europe, and the latter was too deeply prejudiced against Islam and too much interested in fishing in the troubled waters of the Eastern question to allow the Turks to recover the time they had lost.

The policy of the Tsars, and, following in its wake, the whole of European policy adopted as its motto throughout the nineteenth century the "preservation" in a state of weakness of the Ottoman Empire as a precious surety of future benefits, whilst pretending to have a lively interest in the reforms which were to transmute Turkey into a modern state. All the documents to be found in the diplomatic archives of Russia, from the famous letter from Count Kotchoubey to Alexander I. (1802) and the protocol to the secret committee held on the 4th of September, 1829, under the presidency of Nicholas I., which fixed the unchangeable principles of Russian policy with regard to the Turkish efforts at consolidation, to the thesis of Prince Gregory Troubetzkoï, which appeared just after the revolution of 1908, are all agreed on this one point, that a reformed Turkey was inacceptable to the Tsars, who could only tolerate feeble neighbours on the Bosphorus.*

In the face of such designs, what attitude was it possible for Turkey to adopt in order to escape from this death sentence held over her head, however serious her wish for reform might be? She appealed to Western Europe, where she had friends, and twice succeeded, thanks to the support she received, in disengaging herself from the murderous grip of pan-Slavism (1856, 1878), but at the very moment when the reform movement had received its strongest impetus under the guidance of Midhat Pasha, the terrible misfortune overtook her of being subjected to the rule of Abdul Hamid, which cut at the roots

* Serge Gorialnow: *Le Bosphore et les Dardanelles*, Paris, 1910; Gregory Troubetzkoï, *Russland als Grossmacht*, Leipzig, 1910.

of all hope of regeneration. This definite fiasco overtaking the *Tanzimat* for a long time influenced the judgment of Europe in regard to Turkey, a judgment only aggravated by the monstrous nature of the régime which followed and destroyed anything good from the old times that still survived within the Empire.

When the revolution of the Young Turks took in hand the heritage of Abdul Hamid, it was already handicapped by all the political and social evils from which the country is still suffering, and which ended in creating general dissatisfaction in the breasts of those elements least inclined towards separatism. Amongst these evils, the most terrible and deadly for the future of the country was not the Macedonian imbroglio from which the revolution was born ; for the surgical operation which amputated this problem did not by any means reach the vital nerves of the Turkish Empire concentrated in Asia Minor. But the Turco-Armenian problem presented itself in a different and dangerous light. As long as Asia Minor remained a whole, intact in the hands of Turkey, there was a future for Turkey, notwithstanding all the misfortunes that might overtake outlying parts of the huge Empire. But once this whole was seriously encroached upon, all hope of an economic revival was at an end, for the work of reconstruction lacked a geographical base sufficiently rich and extensive to bear the structure of a modern state.

In order to deal the mortal blow to Turkey, who was believed to be in her death agony ever since her defeat in the Balkans, no course appeared more opportune than the reopening of the Armenian question in which the interest of Europe had been revived since the massacres of Abdul Hamid, a question which allowed Tsarism, the accomplice of the Hamidian regime, in 1895, to pose before the public opinion of the world as the protector of a nation which it had helped to strangle twenty years previously. Various circumstances, to which we shall return later, conspired to facilitate this diplomatic game: in the first place the relations between the Kurds and the Armenians, and secondly, the dissatisfaction which had existed ever since 1908 between the new régime in Turkey and the Armenian revolutionaries, a disaffection which the agents of Russia knew well how to turn to account, if they did not actually inspire it.

The Kurdish problem is one of those questions about which the utmost ignorance prevails, although all the accounts of Armenian massacres refer to this primitive race, which has never risen above a tribal organization and is still in the condition in which Xenophon found it four hundred years before the Christian era. Nevertheless it presents one of the most interesting psychological phenomena to be studied in the racial laboratory formed by Asia

Minor. If diplomacy gave the title of Armenia to the six vilayets whose fate preoccupied its attention until the eve of the Great War, it does not mean that from the ethnic point of view the expression is correct. In this so-called Armenia, the Kurdish element, if we can trust the evidence of the statistics published by the French Government in its *Yellow Book* (1893–7), constitutes the majority. According to this publication which was based upon facts provided by the Patriarch of Armenia (but which were always disputed by the Porte) the proportion of Armenians in the six so-called Armenian vilayets of Asia Minor was as follows:

Sivas ...	17%	Kharpout ...	12%
Erzerum ...	30%	Diarbekir ...	17%
Bitlis ...	33%	Van	19%

In the vilayets of Van and Bitlis, where the tension between Kurds and Armenians was at its greatest, the population was divided as follows:

Van.		Bitlis.	
Kurds ...	46 %	Kurds ...	56¾%
Armenians...	27½%	Armenians ...	37¾%
Nestorians	16 %	Various ...	5½%
Various ...	10½%		

The following is the outline of the regions inhabited by Kurds given by Monsieur Zarzecki, a Frenchman, who was for a long time French Consul at Van, and who summed up his experiences in an exceedingly interesting article published in the *Revue de Paris* of April 15th, 1914:

"No more than Armenia does Kurdistan to-day correspond with any precise political division. It is merely a geographical expression designating the district inhabited chiefly by Kurds. This vast tract of country is approximately bounded on the north by a line from Erzindjian, passing through Erzerum and along the Russian frontier as far as Mount Ararat; . . . on the east by a line from Mount Ararat skirting the eastern side of Lake Ourmiah and descending to Kermanchah in Persia; on the south and the west by a line from Kermanchah, passing through Kefri and ascending in the direction of Mossoul, Diarbekir, and Kharpout, and ending at Erzindjian. Within these limits, as you see, a good part of what is called Armenia is also included. Thus Kurdistan and Armenia practically merge into one another, and in certain districts overlap, so that it is very difficult to know where Armenia ends and Kurdistan begins."

Of the two chief ethnic elements inhabiting this geographical area, the most numerous is the Kurdish people, whose numbers are given as follows by the ex-Consul of France:

"Information as to their numbers varies from a given figure to double that number. But if the mean of the different figures is taken, we find that the total number of Kurds is about three millions, of whom two millions are in Turkey, 700,000 in Persia, and 300,000 in Russia. Nevertheless, anyone who has travelled even a little in Kurdistan and studied the extent of the districts occupied by Kurds must come to the conclusion that the above figures are less than the reality."

According to the same authority, the Armenians were, taken altogether, pretty well equal in numbers to the Kurds, but they were more dispersed and only formed a minority in the six vilayets:

"The number of Armenians scattered about the world may be estimated at about 3,000,000, of whom 1,300,000 are in Turkey, 1,100,000 in Russia, 100,000 in Persia, and the rest—about half a million—are divided between America, Egypt, Poland, Rumania, Bulgaria, etc. *Nowhere in Asia Minor do the Armenians exist as a compact national body.* And it is this which constitutes their political weakness and also, it is true, their commercial prosperity, and relegates to the realm of Utopia the dreams of some of them, who number, moreover, exceedingly few, for the reconstitution of a Kingdom of Armenia, which, were it ever realized, it would be exceedingly difficult to know where to place."*

This writer declares that it would be impossible to regard the Kurds as intruders in Armenia. His investigations into the origin of these two peoples

* Even the statistics most favourable to the Armenian element show that nowhere do they constitute a compact majority. Robert de Caix, writing in the *Bulletin du Comité de l'Asie Française*, 1913, p. 11, says "If in Armenia one occasionally comes across Armenian villages, or in the towns, quarters entirely inhabited by Armenians . . . it is much more difficult to find entire districts where Armenians are incontestably in the majority." For details, see Marcel Liart, *La Question Arménienne à la Lumière des Documentés*, Paris, 1913, the Appendices of which print all the statistics relating to the number, the trade, and the education of the Armenians in Turkey. The conclusion to be drawn from these is that, apart from public safety, the Armenians have largely been able to develop their national culture, for in 1902 they possessed 803 schools with 2,088 teachers, 59,513 boys and 27,713 girl scholars. The fact that their trade has always prospered is known to all.

ıave led him to the belief that from the most ancient :imes they have lived side by side and that a close ·elationship existed between the Kurds and at least)ne branch in the ancestry of the Armenians. He ·egards the latter as a mixture of Aryan tribes des-:ending from the plateau of Pamir and Semitic)eoples coming from Mesopotamia. It is probable .hat a close kinship, if not actual identity of race, :xisted between the Kurds and the Aryan element vhich entered into the composition of the Armenian)eople. The languages are very similar, and ety-nologists place the Kurd dialect in the "Armenian ;roup" of Aryan languages. Monsieur Zarzecki even ;oes so far as to formulate the hypothesis that the Kurds in the beginning must have formed a single thnic group with the Armenians; they were the ›oorer brothers of the latter, as their tribes had ahabited mountainous regions and had consequently ıever progressed. They adhered to the customs of ıomads and marauders, whilst the Armenians were ivilized, created kingdoms whose existence, it is rue, was of short duration, and were subjected in urn to the Assyrians, the Medes, the Persians, the ›eleucide Greeks of Syria, the Arabs, the Byzantines, he Mongols, and finally the Turks, all of whom, evertheless, helped them to develop their national ulture. The Kurds, on account of their complete tate of disintegration, have never been able to play part in history. They were easily converted to

Islam, an example which, as a matter of fact, was followed by many Armenians in the mountain districts.

The fact that strikes a conscientious historian, like Monsieur Zarzecki, is that the antagonism between the Kurds and the Armenians only began to show itself under the reign of Abdul Hamid, who incited the tribes who had been converted to Islam against the Christians. Until then it seems probable that no antagonism existed between the two nationalities, although apparently they had lived side by side from time immemorial. And this is sufficient proof of the artificial nature of the conflict in which foreign intervention played no insignificant part.

As for this conflict, it arose from a social and agrarian question, which has assumed a special importance since Europe has interfered in these racial quarrels. In the first place it is not the entire Kurd nation that ill-treats the Armenians, but only a small aristocracy which exploits the peasants without regard to their religious beliefs. Among the latter are a large number of peace-loving Kurds who suffer just as much as the Armenian peasants from the tribal chieftains of the Kurds, who are veritable feudal lords. Despising agricultural labour, these chieftains force the Armenian or Kurd peasants to cultivate their lands for them, giving them a trifling payment in kind. Monsieur Zarzecki, the French ex-Consul at Van, and consequently an observer who enjoyed full opportunities for forming an opinion, tells us that this Kurd aristocracy treated their peasants fairly well, and frequently helped and defended them as necessary collaborators, although they were only serfs. The relationship between the Kurds and the Armenian cultivators of the soil was precisely that of overlord and serf: the Armenians did the work, whilst the Kurds often protected them against each other, when the Armenians in any district were molested by migratory tribes of Kurds.

"Accustomed for centuries to this state of affairs," writes Zarzecki, "the Armenians never dreamed that it could be otherwise, and did not complain of their fate. From the material point of view, moreover, they were not badly off, for after having paid their Kurd 'agha' certain dues, they generally had enough left to live upon. Towards the end of this first period, when the power of the Government had increased at the expense of that of the Kurd chieftains, and especially after the expedition of Osman Pasha to Van, the demands made by the Kurds upon the Armenians became less onerous . . . As a result of this new state of affairs, which was made even more favourable to the Armenians by the promulgation of the *Tanzimat,* larger numbers of Armenians grew rich, and acquired vast properties, many of which were even cultivated by poor Kurd *rayas.*"

It was the régime of Abdul Hamid that upset all this, and substituted permanent hatred and massacres for a condition which, if we bear in mind the primitive degree of civilization reached in these parts, had, on the whole, been tolerable. Let us once more quote the French ex-Consul.

"When the Sultan, urged by the Powers to introduce into Armenia the reforms promised by the Treaty of Berlin, wished to stifle the Armenian question . . . he found zealous supporters in the Kurds. The latter, displeased by the slow but sure progress of the Armenians, and irritated by their revolutionary attempts, obeyed with joy the command . . . to repress the budding movement in Armenia by means of terrorization. And when Abdul Hamid, at the time the Hamidian regiments were formed, gave *carte blanche* to the Kurd *achirets* (tribes) to act as they pleased with regard to the Armenians, the Kurd instinct for brigandage and pillage was given free rein. . . . Thus Abdul Hamid gained his ends by creating between the Kurds and the Armenians, who until then had lived for centuries fairly contentedly together, a permanent under-current of distrust, antagonism and hatred, which was bound only to become accentuated with time, and the disastrous results of which have been obvious for years and constitute one of the causes of the present unsettled condition of the country."

The writer could see but one solution—European control, which seemed to him indispensable on the eve of the War, if the country was to escape occupation by Russia, the danger of which he foresaw. According to him, the majority of Armenians and Kurds would still prefer to remain under Turkish rule, rather than be transferred to that of Russia, the former for national and the latter for religious reasons. On the other hand, racial antagonism, combined with the complete intermingling of the two elements, forbade all thoughts either of a single autonomous Kurdo-Armenian State, or of two separate self-governing States. Monsieur Zarzecki thought it would be sufficient to abolish the privileges of the *achirets* (tribes) beginning with the disbanding of the Hamidian cavalry, and to replace this dangerous organization by the incorporation of the Kurds in the Regular Army.

"After this it would be necessary to settle all questions of disputed territory by appointing a commission of active and honest men to scour the country to examine each case separately and settle it in conformity with the dictates of justice and equity."

The land question is the most fundamental of all those which it is the task of social reform to solve in this country. It is a question of dividing between the peasants, who have for centuries cultivated the lands, the produce of which they have hitherto been obliged to share with the chieftains of the Kurd tribes. The whole of the Kurdo-Armenian question thus resolves itself into an agrarian problem in a country the inhabitants of which have remained in the rudimentary state characteristic of primitive societies. It has always been asserted that Turkey constituted the chief obstacle in the way of a termination of this state of affairs, and that European control or a Russian occupation would provide the most efficacious remedy. But this is merely one of those hackneyed phrases which are used to mask difficulties. Anybody who possesses the smallest knowledge of sociology is aware that a primitive society cannot be changed in a day to meet the requirements of modern economic ideas, and that a mere change of masters is not sufficient, especially if the new master is as altruistic as were the Tsars, to clear away with one sweep of the broom all the evils that have been sedulously maintained by interested parties. If Europe had really desired reforms, instead of making use of them in order to intrigue in the East, she could have made the reform movement in Turkey reach a successful conclusion by merely abstaining from interference. It is a general rule in political matters that reform imposed from outside, without any profound understanding of the country in question, always creates trouble without attaining any practical results. Only such reforms as are carried out from within by people possessing an intimate acquaintance with the daily facts of existence, leave an indelible imprint upon the life of a nation. By a curious coincidence, the chief obstacles which the reform movement had to meet consisted, in addition to the privileged Kurds, of the leaders of the revolutionary organizations of Armenia. These beneficiaries of anarchy feared the inauguration of a state of peace and order for purely personal reasons, which the French ex-Consul sums up in the following words:

"The carrying-out of plans of reform was opposed by two obstacles—the Kurd beys and the leaders of the revolutionary organizations of Armenia. And indeed, the conscientious application of these reforms would, little by little, have abolished the feudal system, and the Kurd beys and aghas would no longer have been able to oppress and exploit the unfortunate peasants living under their control. On the other hand, these same reforms, by securing safety and justice to the Armenian population, would have robbed the Armenian revolutionary leaders of all pretext for interference. They would thus have lost their influence with the masses and would no longer have been able to sell them arms at double their value nor extort money from them on every occasion and for every pretext. Now, since the revolutionary leaders in this country are, as a rule, adventurers, usually of Caucasian origin, incapable of living without carrying on some agitation profitable to themselves, they, like the Kurd beys and aghas, will do all in their power to make schemes of reform prove abortive."*

It is necessary here to say a few words about these Armenian revolutionary organizations. It was largely to their anarchical agitations that the recent massacres were due. Three great political parties rivalled each other for the favours of the Armenian people—Dachnakzoutioun, Hentchakzoutioun, and

* An exceedingly curious document on Kurdo-Armenian relations is to be found in the report of the Russian General, Mayewski, printed by the military press of St. Petersburg and entitled *Statistique des Provinces de Van et de Bitlis*, a report which was designed for the Russian Staff and contains a very severe judgment on the Armenian revolutionaries. This report was translated into French and published in Constantinople at the same time as the Russian original.

Ramgawar-Sahmanatir—and they robbed each other of their partisans by the most violent methods. The Dachnakists until the outbreak of the War constituted the most influential organization, and their leanings towards atheistic socialism which, semi-civilized as they were, they only partially digested, did not prevent them from throwing themselves into the arms of Tsarism when the preparations for joint action between Russia and Armenia gave them an opportunity of "playing a part." On the pretext of having been deceived by the revolution of 1908, in which they had taken part by virtue of an agreement with the Young Turks made in December, 1907, in Paris, and impatient at not seeing their dreams realized, they turned to Russia and were welcomed by her as useful weapons of destruction in the pursuit of her policy of conquest. Thanks to a few misguided ringleaders, like Pastermadjian, Tsarism was thus enabled to lay a hand on the extreme left in Armenia, just as it had succeeded in tying the Armenian Gregorian Church to its apron-strings owing to the complaisance of the Catholicos of Etchmiadzine.

The fact that the "Armenian lambs" in their struggle against the packs of "Kurd wolves" should have aroused the deepest compassion in the breast of Christendom doubtless does great honour to the humanitarian sentiments of Europe and America, though the latter must have been somewhat disillusioned by the spectacle of "civilized" atrocities nearer home. For what are Kurd butcheries compared with those of which Europe was the scene quite recently? The number of Armenians who had their throats cut during forty years was probably less than the number of young men mown down in Europe in forty days of a single "great offensive." The argument that Europe was then in an exceptional state of war is not to the point, for the Kurds might retort that their country has not even yet emerged from that state of social warfare out of which all societies have been born. The Kurd tribes who rob and kill have no pretensions to civilization; they do so from custom or from hatred, with the single object of living their own lives. To cure them of these unpraiseworthy habits, it is not sufficient to preach European morality to them; they should be taught the advantages of a sedentary and agricultural existence, and settled by the distribution of uncultivated but fertile lands to encourage in them a taste for a peaceful life. This is a task which could only be accomplished by an independent Musulman Government, since the Kurds form a part of Islam; foreign intervention would do nothing but aggravate the evil, as all experience has proved.

The astonishing fact is that statesmen whose position should have led them to study the Armenian question, nearly always contented themselves with the hackneyed explanations provided by the Press, instead of taking the trouble to give a little time and study to a problem, with the solution of which they professed to deal. In the majority of the publications on Armenia which appeared both before and during the War, there is not the slightest trace of the real issues of the problem. If one refers to so important a document as the English Blue Book on Armenian affairs,* edited by that great scholar and diplomatist, Lord Bryce, one is struck by the absence of any attempt to probe to the core of the problem. Descriptions and evidence about the massacres do not exhaust the subject; for these massacres were only the symptoms (and the consequences) of a deep-seated evil, which is not explained by the accusation brought by Lord Bryce against the Turks, those hydra-headed Turks whom other Englishmen continued to describe in the *Times* as "gentlemen," even after their experience of them during the War!† Yet England cannot complain of a lack of distinguished Orientalists fully capable of enlightening the Foreign Office regarding the true aspects of problems, which the latter aspires to solve in the interests of humanity.

Sir Mark Sykes, in his book, *The Caliph's Last*

* *The Treatment of Armenians in the Ottoman Empire*, 1915–16, p. 684.

† See *The Times* of the 20th March, 1917, as also the declarations previously published of General Townsend, who was captured at Kut-el-Amara by the Turks.

*Heritage,** describes the intractable nature of the races which inhabit Asia Minor and gives the following account of the character of the Armenian revolutionaries:

"In common with many others of the Christians of Turkey, the town Armenians have an extraordinarily high opinion of their own capacities; but in their case this is combined with a strongly unbalanced judgment, which permits them to proceed to lengths that invariably bring trouble on their heads. They will undertake the most desperate political crimes . . . they will bring ruin and disaster on themselves and others without any hesitation; they will overthrow their national cause to vent some petty spite on a private individual . . . they will suddenly abandon all hope when their plans are nearing fruition; they will betray the very person who might serve their cause. . . . That the Armenians are doomed to be for ever unhappy as a nation seems to me unavoidable, for one half of their miseries arises not from the stupid, cranky, ill-managed despotism under which they live but from their own dealings with each other. In a time of famine at Van, the Armenian merchants tried to corner the available grain; the Armenian revolutionaries prefer to plunder their co-religionists to giving battle to their enemies; the anarchists of Constantinople threw bombs with the intention of provoking a massacre of their fellow-countrymen. The Armenian villages are divided against themselves; the revolutionary societies are leagued against one another; the

* Sir Mark Sykes, *The Caliph's Last Heritage*, London, Macmillan, 1915, pp. 405 and 415. See also an analysis of this work by Marmaduke Pickthall in *La Revue Politique Internationale*, May–June, 1916.

priests connive at the murder of a bishop ; the Church is divided at its very foundations."

" As for the tactics of the revolutionaries, anything more fiendish one could not imagine—the assassination of Moslims in order to bring about the punishment of innocent men, the midnight extortion of money from villages which have just paid their taxes by day, the murder of persons who refuse to contribute to their collection boxes, are only some of the crimes of which Moslims, Catholics, and Gregorians accuse them with no uncertain voice."

And Sir Mark Sykes further states on the evidence of investigations made from time to time in Asia Minor, that the situation between Musulmans and Christians is becoming more and more intolerable. He writes :

" Fifty years of rational education might possibly redeem them. But I cannot see how it will end. The forcible deportation of one party or the other is the only remedy that I can think of. The mollahs and the missionaries would have to be put under lock and key before any serious reforms could be undertaken."

He, furthermore, agrees that modern civilization, badly understood and hastily applied, introduces more evils into these primitive countries than it cures. What they lack above all is security, and to obtain this it is quite useless to disturb the whole map of Asia Minor. Regarded closely, the whole problem can be reduced to the creation of a strong police force capable of maintaining order, and punishing all disturbers of the peace without distinction of race or religion, under the protection of which force, social and agrarian reforms could be carried out without trouble.*

IV

In these troubles, which periodically degenerated into organized massacres, the local officials, forgetful of their duties or else corrupted by the beneficiaries of disorder, no doubt played their sinister part. The principal wound in the side of the Ottoman Empire, aggravated by the outrageous methods of the régime of Abdul Hamid, which was prolonged for thirty years owing to the support of Russia and the whole of European diplomacy, was the fact that it possessed no honest officials in the various departments of the imperial edifice. The revolution of 1908 was not able to remedy this evil in the comparatively short space of time at its disposal. It must be borne in mind, moreover, that the deepest interests of the Great Powers were all in favour of the maintenance of corruption, from which they were the first to profit, and further that some among them were not exactly qualified to pose as Doctors of Administrative Integrity . . . But this is not the place to embark upon a comparative study of corruption in the

* Sir Mark Sykes' book contains a table of the Kurd tribes in the Ottoman Empire, Appendix, pp. 553–88.

various states of the two worlds, or to slur over the responsibility incurred by the old Turkish officials, who were veritable scourges to their own people as well as to all the other races within the Empire. The demoralization caused by so many years of despotism has left upon the country a mark which ten years of revolutionary measures have not been able entirely to efface on account of the incessant struggles which have taken place during that time for the very preservation of the State itself. The internal revolution was constantly attacked by attempts from without to execute the death sentence, which, according to the physicians of the Eastern question, Turkey was not on any account to be allowed to escape. The political revolution has been accomplished more or less successfully, but the social revolution of which Islam stands so much in need must be postponed to better days, when the very existence of the last independent Musulman Power in the world is no longer called in question.

It was Russia, more than all the other Powers, who had a capital interest in putting a spoke in the wheel of the Turkish revolution. For her, the rejuvenation of the last Islamic state and the consolidation of the Ottoman Empire was inacceptable on principle, and it was with some displeasure that she saw public opinion in the West unanimously saluting the revolution of 1908 as the work of a spirit capable of regenerating the East. Whilst the grave mistakes made by these inexperienced revolutionaries during the early days of the new régime did much to account for the complete change of opinion in Europe with regard to them, the sincerity of their efforts can never be doubted, as is proved by the evidence of even those who have criticized them most.* At all events, the alacrity with which Russia and, in her wake, the whole of European diplomacy profited from mistakes which are common to every revolution, in order to revive their policy of destruction against Young Turkey also, without allowing her the time required to solve the weighty problems which complicated the legacy she had received from Abdul Hamid, this eagerness to discredit the Turkish revolution in the eyes of public opinion, although consummate patience had been shown towards the tyranny of the ex-Sultan, shows how little sincere was the welcome accorded by the *Governments* to the events of 1908. The *peoples* of Europe had a confused feeling that here was one last attempt to save them from the general conflagration which was smouldering in the East, an attempt, moreover, to save them by the most efficacious means—the raising of the Turkish people who, after so many centuries of isolation, were ready to join the other nations in the struggle of progress. And this explains the general popularity of the

* André Mandelstam in the Russian Review, *Roussyia Mysl*, Moscow, 1916.

revolution of 1908, the leaders of which found the warmest welcome wherever they went in Europe. But the agents of the Tsar were keeping watch ; for their trade the light which had appeared in the East was not a favourable omen, for, on the one hand, they feared the spread of the revolution to the Musulmans of the Caucasus, and, on the other, they dreaded the moral effect of the regeneration of Turkey upon the Christians in the East. With her eyes turned towards Constantinople, Russia required a conflagration in order to roast her chestnuts. Thanks to the blind complicity of European diplomacy, she succeeded in setting it alight.

The final aim of Russia was perfectly clear ; she wanted to "adopt towards the Armenians the policy which had failed with Bulgaria," and one day to reach the Bosphorus by the circuitous route along the northern coast of the Black Sea, since the independence of Bulgaria had closed the direct road to Constantinople against her.* The covetous designs of Russia can always be explained by the same *leitmotif*—the search for access to the open sea, which, in the case of the Armenian question, drew her to the Gulf of Alexandretta. It is only necessary to cast a glance at the map to understand the strategic importance of so-called Turkish Armenia ; the lofty plateau of Erzerum forms, by the

* René Pinon, *La Turquie d'Asie et les Provinces Arméniennes* (*Bulletin du Comité de l'Asie Française*, 1913, p. 294).

very configuration of the soil a most formidable fortress, especially in the hands of a world Power like Russia, who would use it as a gate opening on to the rest of Asia Minor and into Mesopotamia, in order to secure a dominating position for herself. This was the aim which Imperial Russia had always had in view ever since she had seized Transcaucasia, and it was in full consciousness of this objective that she tied the Catholicos of Etchmiadzine to her apron strings in the nineteenth century, and that she kept in touch with the Armenians and the Kurds, both of whom were equally "valuable" for the maintenance of disorder in Asia Minor. If, for over a century, the policy of England was directed towards checking these manœuvres, it was because she realized the danger they constituted to the road to India. Whilst awaiting the day for this opposition on the part of England to be broken, it was important for Russia not to allow these agitated districts to be pacified, so that, at the opportune moment, she might appear as the protector of the liberties of the weak and down-trodden, a policy which had served her in good stead in the case of Poland in the eighteenth century. Knowing, before the Anglo-Russian agreement of 1907, that this moment had not yet arrived, she for a long time allowed the Armenophobe policy of her Governors in Tiflis free play, not for the mere gratification of the whims of a Grand Duke or a Prince Galitzine, but with the object, openly avowed by Prince Lobanoff-Rostowski, of "ridding Armenia of Armenians." When, in the domain of diplomacy, the groups of alliances had removed the principal obstacle to Russian designs, the Armenians, according to Monsieur René Pinon's phrase, took the place of the Bulgars in the calculations of the Tsar, who now posed as their chief protector against Turkey.

From that time forward Russian agents intensified their double-faced activities in Asia Minor. It was necessary, on the one hand, to create a pretext for the proposed intervention of the Tsar, and, on the other, to make international public opinion which was interested in the fate of the Armenians, believe that the latter actually desired his protection. To provide a pretext it was sufficient to stir up the antagonism between Kurds and Armenians. The Russian consulates in the six so-called Armenian vilayets were provided with arms and munitions, which they distributed among the revolutionaries, not forgetting the Kurds, who were quite ready to march with Russia out of hatred of the new régime in Turkey, which had tried to abolish their privileges in favour of the Armenians. This double game was duly exposed by English travellers who visited Asia Minor just after the Balkan War in order to conduct an inquiry. Thus Mr. Walter Guinness, a Member of Parliament, made a prolonged stay among the Armenians and the Kurds towards the end of the year 1913, and published the results of his investigations in the *National Review*.* After showing that, in the five years following the Turkish revolution, the relations between Musulmans and Christians had greatly improved, and that credit was due to Turkey for this, Mr. Guinness expressed anxiety (remember he was writing six months before the War) regarding the numerous indications of active propaganda on the part of Russia. What struck him most was not so much the intimacy between the Russian consulates and the Armenian revolutionaries—an intimacy of which he was aware—but the novel relationship between Russia and the Kurds. He writes:

"More remarkable is the liking which Kurds show for Russia. Although they are very free from any form of Turkish influence, and the obligation of military service is most imperfectly enforced, Kurds hate the Turks. Many of them are armed with Russian rifles, and in an inaccessible mountain village I found a Russian dressed as a Kurd and living the Kurdish life. He was said to have been there for some years and to have left Russia owing to trouble with the Russian police. This may have been true; on the other hand, I was informed that he travelled frequently to the capital of the vilayet and received money from his brother, who was a Russian officer. It was at least remarkable that such a man should choose to spend his life in a particularly dirty Kurdish village unless for some strong reason." †

* Walter Guinness, *Impressions of Armenia and Kurdistan*, *National Review*, January, 1914.
† Walter Guinness, *op. cit.*

These activities on the part of Russia which had aroused the suspicions of the English Member of Parliament, were explained later on irrefutable evidence. In the month of April, 1913, when rumours were again abroad of a forthcoming Armenian massacre, and the Russian Government was raising the alarm in the whole European Press by quoting "disquieting" telegrams from its consuls in Erzerum, Van, and other places in Turkish Armenia, the head of a French religious mission to Mossoul imparted a curious fact to his friends in Paris. The chiefs of several Kurd tribes had met at that date in order to discuss whether they would "march" with Russia, who was inciting them to create trouble with the object of preparing the way for Russian intervention planned for that moment. A certain man named Rezak, the son of a Kurd Pasha, and an old favourite of Abdul Hamid, whom the Turks had condemned to death on account of his innumerable acts of brigandage, but had never been able to catch, went over to the service of Russia and set to work as an *agent-provocateur* among the Kurds. Between Tiflis and the districts about Lake Ourmiah, where the ringleaders supporting the policy of Russia were safe from Turkish justice, there was at this time a perpetual traffic connected with the preparation of the troubles which were to facilitate the intervention of Russia. It has been proved that Rezak and his associates were received by the Russian authorities at Tiflis ; later on they were seen showing themselves off with the presents they had received from Vorontzoff-Dachkoff, the Governor-General of the Caucasus, and the traces of their sinister activities among the Kurds were proved. And it was the French missionaries who interfered in 1913 to prevent the massacres counted upon by the Government of Nicholas II., whose ambassadors were already " working " the Cabinets of Europe, in order to persuade them to entrust to the Tsar the task of protecting the Christians of Asia Minor.

And, indeed, nothing would better have served the purposes of Russia in Asia Minor than a fresh series of Kurdo-Armenian massacres, which would have alarmed Europe, deprived the Young Turks of the last vestiges of sympathy they still possessed in the eyes of English public opinion, and imposed Russian intervention as a benefit to Christendom. The Turkophile element in political circles in Great Britain, reinforced by a similar element among the Musulmans of India, happened just at that moment to have founded an Anglo-Turkish Committee in London, under the presidency of Lord Lamington, which tried to oppose the destructive influence of Russia in the East. The Balkan War gave rise to grave anxiety among the Musulmans within the British Empire, and the Moslim League of Young Indians raised a strong agitation on account of the abandonment of Turkey by the Foreign Office at the most critical moments. Englishmen who adhered to the Oriental traditions of Lord Beaconsfield were still fairly numerous and did not cease to make their voices heard in the Press and in Parliament. Mr. Bryce, during a debate on the East in March, 1913, in the House of Commons, drew attention to the danger of Russian intervention. He said:

> "There are indications to show that the Armenians have seriously appealed for Russian intervention. . . . Supposing the Armenians are forced to ask for protection, shall we oppose the demand that Russia will make to carry out reforms?"

Behind this prudent formula we can already perceive the fear of the disorders that might break out in the six vilayets. The Russian consuls at Erzerum and Van periodically gave warning of the danger, and Monsieur Sazonow, the Russian Minister for Foreign Affairs, hastened to convey their prophecies to the Cabinets of Europe. They professed to fear the consequences of the settlement in Asia Minor of the *mouhadjirs* (Musulman *émigrés* who had been driven from Turkey in Europe by the Balkan War) whom the Porte provided with work. Nevertheless, it was pointed out in the English Parliament by Mr. Acland, the Under-Secretary of State for Foreign Affairs, during the same debate in 1913, that the settlement of these unfortunate refugees in Asia Minor presented no danger whatever to the Armenians. In answer to Mr. Bryce and Mr. O'Connor, Mr. Acland declared:

"We have a Consul at Adana who keeps us constantly informed, and I am happy to say that the few hundreds of refugees and their families who have arrived from Europe in this part of Asia Minor have been successfully settled there and that work has been found for them, often among the Armenian population. The rumours of difficulties have been greatly exaggerated and the Armenians up to the present have enjoyed perfect safety and no difficulty has arisen."

In the same speech, Mr. Acland promised the House of Commons to see to it that the Armenian question was discussed by all the Cabinets together and that no Power took isolated action. In May of the same year, Sir Edward Grey, in his general survey of foreign affairs, made a discreet allusion to a "cause for anxiety," due to the possibility of disorders and massacres in the Asiatic provinces of Turkey, an anxiety which occupied the attention of those political circles in England who wished a political question to be raised regarding Asia Minor.

These mysterious allusions veiled the anxiety felt by England at seeing Russia taking up the Armenian question and turning to her own account the troubles of which it was easy for her to warn Europe, since she was directly connected with them, in order to proceed to a military occupation of the six vilayets. The preparations for such action were only too obvious.

Ever since the reception of the Catholicos of Etchmiadzine by the Tsar in the summer of 1912 the Armenian question had been placed by Russian diplomacy in the same category as the Macedonian question. It was a matter of creating in Asia Minor a new "Macedonia," complete in every detail, since Macedonia in Europe had been taken from Turkey in the autumn of 1912 by the Balkan Confederation, the close connexion of which with Russia is to-day a duly established historical fact.* But to attack Turkey from the front without planting a knife in her back would not have been in keeping with Russian methods, which can easily find instruments able to carry out such a task. What could be easier than to set the Armenians and the Kurds at each others' throats by making life equally insupportable for both, so that they would beg for the "deliverance" that Russia would bring them on the day that international contingencies allowed her to do so! The Catholicos of Etchmiadzine was entrusted with "preparing" public opinion in Armenia, for it was essential to impress Europe with the almost complete unanimity with which the Armenians would place their destinies in the hands of Nicholas II. It was for this purpose that Boghos Noubar Pasha, a rich Egyptian Armenian, and the delegate of the Catholicos, appeared in Europe, and went from one capital to the other in order to prepare the way for the action

* See Guéchoff, *L'Alliance Balkanique*, Paris, Hachette.

of Russia. The founder of *L'Union Générale Arménienne de Bienfaisance* in Cairo, in close touch with all the Armenian organizations of Europe, with the secret societies founded in 1887 in London and Paris, with the British Armenia Committee (the founder of which was Count Loris-Melikoff, and the President the Member of Parliament, Mr. Aneurin Williams) affiliated to the Armenophile Committee of the German Lepsius; Boghos Noubar Pasha placed himself at the head of a "National Delegation" appointed by the Catholicos, Kervork V., and raised the Armenian problem before public opinion in Europe.

If he had confined himself to making an appeal to public opinion alone, carefully avoiding all contact with such avowed detractors of Turkey as Monsieur Iswolski, the Russian Ambassador in Paris, he would have been more sympathetically received in Constantinople, where (if we may believe the testimony of one so highly placed as Sir Edward Grey, who made reassuring assertions on this subject in Parliament in May, 1913), the necessity for reform was perfectly well understood. When, on the 12th of May, 1913, the Armenian National Assembly laid a petition before the Grand Vizier, calling his attention to the dangerous condition of the six vilayets, Mahmoud Chefket Pasha replied:

"The Armenians are not the only people to suffer from brigandage, others are also suffering from it.

The Government is firmly resolved to put an end to all such crimes. Too many speeches have been delivered, and too many promises made. I shall avoid making promises; the Government will declare itself by acts."*

One such act, which might have reassured all those who were well-disposed, had just been performed by this Government in the spring of 1913, at the time of the revolt of Bitlis. A band of Kurds, bribed by the Russian consul at Bitlis, had tried to provoke the massacre of Armenians in that town, which Monsieur Sazonow, on information received from his consuls in Asia Minor, had warned the Cabinets of Europe, would take place. These massacres were to be the signal for the intervention of the Tsar, but they were nipped in the bud by the Porte, who got wind of the affair, and hastened to concentrate in Bitlis a sufficient force of police, so as to be ready at the slightest sign of trouble. The Kurd rebels were reduced to impotence before they were able to cut the throat of a single Armenian, but their leader took refuge with the Russian consul, who had been his accomplice and the organizer of the whole business. The danger of intervention was for the time being postponed, but the Russian consul was not punished by his Government, although Monsieur Sazonow, for the sake of appearances, had him disowned and recalled from

* René Pinon, *op. cit., Bulletin du Comité de L'Asie Française National Review*, 1913, p. 293.

Bitlis for having been so clumsy as to be caught in the act.*

It is impossible to over-emphasize the importance of the revolt of Bitlis, for if it had succeeded, the European War would have taken place a year earlier. If Armenian massacres, subsidized by the agents of the Tsar, had broken out at that moment, by leading to the inevitable intervention of Russia, a general European war would, without any doubt, have been provoked by the Armenian question, which would have raised all the other problems connected with Asia Minor. In this contingency Mahmoud Chefket Pasha rendered a real service to Europe by the energy he displayed in checking the machinations of Russia.

Nevertheless, knowing the real intentions of the latter, neither Mahmoud Chefket, who was assassinated a few weeks later, nor his successor was able to refrain from an instinctive feeling of suspicion with regard to the proceedings of Boghos Noubar Pasha who relied on the good intentions of such a Government. It is true that the envoy of the Catholicos hastened to deny the " political object " of which he was accused, declaring that " independence and self-government could never be regarded as a solution " and that the " National Delegation " had never

* If any doubt the authenticity of such an affair, let me remind them that it was brought to the notice of the House of Commons, and that several Members of Parliament knew of it at the time it occurred.

dreamed of any such thing " on account of the ethnic and geographical position of the Armenian vilayets."* But what weight could be attached to such verbal assurances when deeds proved the contrary? The intimate connexion that bound the Armenian agitators to Russia and to her most notorious representatives, such as Monsieur Iswolski, was proved by Monsieur Michel Pavlovitch, a Russian Socialist writer, who revealed the importance of it. He writes:

> " At the instigation of the Catholicos a conference was held in Paris in February, 1913, on the question of reforms in Turkish Armenia. The Catholicos only took the responsibility for this step after having been assured of the approval of the Russian Government. . . . Monsieur Iswolski had a whole series of interviews with the members of this conference . . . who took up the attitude that *the Armenian question could only be solved by Russia*. . . . In accordance with this point of view a plan of reform was drawn up by Bishop Yatiouchane, one of the members of the Conference, a plan which was introduced into Turkey under the ægis of the Russian Government. . . and of which the principal clause was self-government for Armenia *under the protectorate of Russia*." †

What did this mean if not the detachment from Turkey of the six vilayets, a stretch of country representing a third of Asia Minor? And the way in which the Russo-Armenian action was carried out

* *Bulletin du Comité de l'Asie Française*, June, 1913, p. 297.
† Michel Pavlovitch, *La Russie et les Arméniens*, *op. cit.*, p. 472.

was not calculated to inspire confidence in the words of Boghos Noubar Pasha, when he declared himself a supporter of the integrity of the Ottoman Empire, although he allowed himself to be inspired by Monsieur Iswolski. All his dealings with the Cabinets of Europe, in Paris as well as in London, in Berlin and in Rome, were merely calculated to win the consent of the whole of Europe to the Russian control of the six vilayets, an object in which he was supported not only by the "British Armenia Committee," but also by the *Deutsche Orient Mission* under Dr. Lepsius. In the *Réunion Internationale Arménienne*, organized in Paris by the *Comité de l'Asie Française* on the 30th of November, 1913, under the presidency of General Lacroix, two Germans, Lepsius and Rohrbach, inspired by the *Wilhelmstrasse*, declared themselves in favour of this action. Lepsius even went so far as to pronounce himself in favour of a Russian occupation.* The Germans at that time were anxious to show solicitude for the Armenians, lest the other Powers should succeed in securing their own influence in a matter so important for the future of the East. The English Members of Parliament, O'Connor, Whyte, and Williams, rivalled Milioukoff in their desire to "protect" these unfortunate people, whose misery was to serve the most selfish ends of

* See the account of this "meeting" in the *Bulletin du Comité de l'Asie Française*, November, 1912. On the subject of Lepsius, see p. 455.

European policy. The two Buxton brothers, who had just made a tour of Asia Minor, unconsciously played the game of the Tsar, Harold Buxton openly declaring that "if Russian troops crossed the frontier, they would be welcomed as friends, as liberators."*

If we give up juggling with words, this could mean nothing else but *annexation* by Russia. Yet Mr. Bryce a few months previously, in his speech early in 1913 already quoted, had declared that "the Armenians did not desire annexation by Russia, as they wished to preserve the national and individual character of their Church and knew that under Russian domination they could not hope to keep either the one or the other." And in the *Bulletin du Comité de l'Asie Française,* which had never ceased discussing the Armenian question ever since it had been raised when the Balkan War was in full swing, a Frenchman, Monsieur Ludovic de Contenson, uttered words of wisdom:

"Annexation by Russia," he said, "is a solution which, from despair of their cause, a few Armenians may desire . . . but it would mean the end without appeal of the Armenian nation, for, as is always the way, it would quickly be Russianized by force and would see its language and religion more or less energetically opposed, as has already happened with the Armenians in Russia. Order, security, prosperity and peace under Russia would doubtless be secured to the Armenians,

* *Op. cit.*, p. 456.

but would not these benefits have been too dearly bought by the *definite loss of their national soul?* "*

As a matter of fact, even the immediate introduction of the most efficacious reforms into the six vilayets would not have disarmed Russia against Turkey. When at Berlin the latter asked for a new military mission to reconstruct the Turkish army, which had been disorganized by the Balkan War, and Germany sent General Liman von Sanders in November, 1913. Russia lodged an energetic protest against this attempt to consolidate Turkey, demanding as " compensation " that a police force under the command of Russian officers should be stationed in the six vilayets. After her experiences at the time of the revolt of Bitlis, it would have meant veritable suicide for Turkey to consent to this proposal. In Paris the significance of the demand was perfectly well understood, and the *Comité de l'Asie Française* did not attempt to blind themselves to the " consequences to which such a policy was bound sooner or later to lead for the Ottoman Empire." They knew, and even put into writing, that " if Turkey adopted an attitude which Russia regarded as inacceptable, it would be very easy for the latter, even if a pretence were made of introducing reforms in Armenia, to provoke disorders in that country which would facilitate an intervention upheld by the support of

* Ludovic de Contenson. *La Question Arménienne*, 1913, *op. cit.*, p. 15.

the Christian element."* It was impossible to convey in clearer terms to Turkey that unless she submitted to the will of the Tsar she was condemned to death.

V

There are people who are astonished that Turkey did not wish to die, but preferred to ally herself to the devil in order to escape the fate mapped out for her. At one time she hoped to win the support of England, who had already saved her from the claws of pan-Slavism in 1878. By the Convention of Cyprus of the 4th of June, 1878, England had undertaken to guarantee the integrity of the Asiatic possessions of Turkey in exchange for the island of Cyprus, which Lord Beaconsfield thought would provide him with a base for bringing pressure to bear on any Power menacing Asia Minor. The Young Turks, wishing to give a guarantee of their sincerity on the subject of reforms, addressed themselves directly to the Foreign Office and asked for English technical experts for the six vilayets. And they based their request on the Convention of Cyprus, which contained a clause on the subject of British collaboration in reform. Sir Edward Grey accepted the request on principle, but after a little while it became clear that he was not in a position to do any-

* *Bulletin du Comité de l'Asie Française*, 1913, p. 484.

thing to meet it. To a question asked in the House of Commons on the 1st of July, 1913, he replied through his Under Secretary of State, Mr. Acland, that the demand for English technical experts for Asia Minor had indeed emanated from the Porte, but that circumstances required a "study" of the question before any definite reply could be given. The visit of Monsieur Poincaré to London about this date enabled the matter to be deliberated with France, and whether the President were the envoy of the Tsar, or whether the latter brought direct pressure to bear in London, the fact remains that the question was shelved. Russia, who reserved the six vilayets to herself as her "sphere of influence," and obtained the tacit consent of the Great Powers to this proceeding, had every motive for preventing the appointment of English technical experts in the six vilayets, which she reserved for her own candidates. Lord Milner was mentioned, and Mr. Robert Graves, and others to whom Turkey would have been ready to give full powers for carrying out the work of reform, provided they were not agents bound to the Tsar. In the *Times* of the 26th of November, 1913, Djavid openly declared: "We will not allow Armenia to be turned into a second Macedonia," adding that, if political influences prevented Turkey from obtaining the help of distinguished technical experts from England or France, she would appeal to neutral Powers rather than submit to the demands of Russia.

What, from the psychological point of view, could be more natural than this fundamental mistrust that the policy of the Tsar inspired in the breasts of the Turks! Nevertheless they made yet one final attempt to induce Russia to consent to their preservation as a nation. The Russo-Turkish negotiations which lasted for several months between Monsieur Giers, the Russian Ambassador at Constantinople, and Djavid Bey, the Minister of Finance, were finally broken off owing to the impossible demands of Russia. The Young Turks then made a direct appeal to the Tsar by sending a special mission to Livadia in May, 1914, three months before the outbreak of war. This special embassy, under the leadership of Talaat, tried to persuade the Tsar that Turkey wished for nothing better than to be able to become the friend of a pacific Russia, on condition that she would allow Turkey *to live*. With reference to this step, Monsieur Sazonow himself was obliged to confess, in his speech of the 23rd of May in the Duma, that "conversations with the members of this special mission had impressed him with the serious desire of Turkey to establish relations with Russia which should be in keeping with the interests of both countries and with the new political conditions."[1] This action on the part of the Turks, who almost begged the Tsar to refrain from a policy which meant certain death to their country, was further emphas-

[1] *Bulletin du Comité de l'Asie Française*, May, 1914, p. 181.

ized by the creation of a Committee in Constantinople for the betterment of Russo-Turkish relations. All in vain! Russia was by no means disposed to loosen her grip, believing that now at last she had a firm hold on her prey, thanks to the support of the whole of European diplomacy, which, ever since the Balkan War, had made her the arbiter of the East.

Germany herself was on the point of joining the ranks of those who wished to hasten the partition of the Ottoman Empire. The battle of Lulé-Bourgas, in November, 1912, created a veritable anti-Turkish current in German diplomacy, a current which reached the *Wilhelmstrasse* in the person of Herr Kiderlen-Wächter, who was then Secretary of State for Foreign Affairs. Kiderlen-Wächter and his friends believed that it was impossible to bolster up Turkey against the wishes of two Great Powers so deeply interested in the Eastern question as Russia and Great Britain, and that thenceforward it would be better to come to some agreement with them for the partition of the spoil. By this means they hoped to obtain for their own country a large part of the heritage of Turkey. The only consideration which finally prevailed against this point of view, especially after the death of Kiderlen-Wächter, was the objection that even if a partition profitable to Germany were made, she would not be able to keep her prey for long, because, in order to reach that part of the East which would be allotted to her, " she would be obliged to stretch across seas and straits, and all round Europe, an unconscionably long thin arm."* Nevertheless, at the time the Armenian question was raised by Russia in the spring of 1913, German diplomacy had not yet decided to support Turkey in case of war. Supposing the revolt of the Kurds in Bitlis in the month of April, 1913, had not been promptly stifled by the Porte, and that, in consequence of fresh massacres of Armenians, the Russian army had intervened, as it wished to do, is it to be supposed that Germany would have risked a world war rather than raise the question of "compensations" in St. Petersburg? At all events, the question of peace or war depended at that moment on the Armenian question, which thus assumes exceptional importance in diplomatic history.

The Russian Government itself published the most convincing document that could possibly be required for basing the judgment of history regarding its machinations in the East on the eve of the war. To prove to the Armenians the profound interest it took in them, it published in Russian and Armenian the whole of the diplomatic correspondence relating to the Armenian problem. In a voluminous pamphlet destined exclusively for the Armenian public, it even inserted the protocol of the confi-

* Paul Rohrbach, *L'Evolution de l'Allemagne comme Puissance Mondiale, Revue Politique Internationale*, July, 1914, p. 32.

dential deliberations of the Commission called *The Commission of Yenikeuy*, composed of representatives of the various embassies in Constantinople, which met in the month of July, 1914, in the summer palace of the Austro-Hungarian Ambassador, to discuss the plans of Russia with regard to the Armenians. This compilation appeared in 1915 in Tiflis written in the Armenian language and contains a host of interesting matter.*

Hardly had the Balkan War taken a turn unfavourable to the Turks, in November, 1912, than Russian diplomacy hastened to mobilize the Armenians in order to prepare the mortal blow against the dying Empire. On the 21st of November, 1912, a report from the Russian Vice-Consul at Van announced that "all the Armenians are in favour of Russia and sincerely desire the advent of Russian soldiers, or reforms under the supervision of Russia." On the same date the Vice-Consul of Bayazid telegraphed to Giers, the Ambassador of the Tsar at Constantinople:

> "All the Armenians, without distinction of party, are entirely hostile to Turkey and ardently desire the suzerainty of Russia *and the occupation of Armenia.*"

Giers quoted the appeal of the Catholicos of Etchmiadzine to the Viceroy of the Caucasus, begging for the intervention of the Tsar, an appeal

* *Les Réformes en Arménie* (12th of November, 1912, to the 10th of May, 1914), translated by the jurisconsult Setrak Avakian, Tiflis, 1915. (There is a French translation in manuscript.)

which, according to him, exactly expressed the attitude of Turkish Armenia towards Russia. In his telegrams to Sazonow, Giers emphasized the capital importance of the problem raised by the religious head of the Armenian people in conformity with the view of Russia. He expressed a fear lest Russia should let slip this unique opportunity of taking the initiative regarding intervention, and recommended Sazonow to give assurances to the Catholicos and the Patriarch of Constantinople, as well as "all possible support." It was a matter of preventing the Armenians from turning to the Great Powers, although the occupation of the six vilayets desired by many Armenians seemed to him "premature." For the time being he would be content with "certain reforms in Turkish territory, carried out under the control of Russian agents, *hoping that these reforms would have no result, but that it would be necessary to send a Russian army to the above-mentioned provinces*."*

In replying to his Ambassador, Sazonow informed him of the petition of the Catholicos of the 30th November, 1912, and threatened Turkey with European intervention, adding that "the outbreak of troubles in the provinces adjoining our frontiers would be of a nature to compromise our relations with Turkey by leading to insoluble complications." In order to ensure these complications thus amiably

* The Tiflis Records (in Armenian), Document No. 1.

predicted, Giers entered into confidential communication with the Turkish Armenians and kept his staff well informed. In December he announced that the Armenian Committees in London and Paris had appealed to the English and French Governments to beg for the combined protection of the Great Powers, or else the entrusting of the Armenian question to the hands of the Tsar. As for the National Armenian Delegation which was to visit Europe, Giers asked that the initiative should be reserved for Russia.* Sazonow on his side informed his Ambassadors in Europe, in a confidential letter dated 13th December, 1912, that a number of Turkish Armenians were begging the Russian Government to occupy "certain districts" in Asia Minor. He suggested an immediate exchange of views with the Cabinets of London and Paris "in order to put a stop to any united conclusions or concerted actions," and he asked the two Governments to advise their Ambassadors in Constantinople to support the views of the Russian Ambassador.†

Meanwhile the Porte had drawn up a general plan of reform instituting in the six so-called Armenian vilayets two new administrative sections, each of which would have at its head an Inspector-General, as well as a council composed of two Armenians and two Europeans under the presidency of a third

* The Tiflis Records, Documents Nos. 2–4.
† *Ibid.*, Document No. 5.

European. Giers thought it would be desirable to see some Russians among the European members.

Towards Christmas, Dr. Zavrieff, a delegate belonging to the Dachnakzoutioun party, who in 1907 had already sent to the Russian Government a memorandum on the Armenian question, declared to Giers that " the general belief among Armenians is that their future depends upon Russia," from whom they were awaiting instructions as to the attitude they should adopt towards Turkey. Zavrieff openly asked for the intervention of Russia.* The Patriarch was not satisfied with the Turkish plan of reform which would have replaced European control by Europeans in the service of Turkey, and demanded guarantees from either Russia or the Great Powers. Giers telegraphed to Sazonow that " Russian occupation is regarded by the Armenians as the most efficacious form of guarantee." The meeting of the national assembly of Armenia held on the 21st of December (old style), 1912, proved the complete solidarity of all parties in Armenia in favour of Russia.†

The Armenians in Europe were very active at this time and were trying to win over the corps of Ambassadors in London to their cause, which was far from pleasing to the Viceroy of the Caucasus, who was anxious to reserve the protection of Armenia for

* The Tiflis Records ; Document No. 7.

† *Ibid.*, Documents Nos. 8, 11.

Russia alone. He telegraphed to Sazonow that the Catholicos advised Boghos Noubar Pasha, his envoy in Europe, not to appeal to the Ambassadors' Conference in London, but to confine his activities to preparing the ground for Russian intervention. At the same time he announced that troubles would shortly break out in Anatolia, a subject on which he was well informed, since he himself had arranged for them.*

In the telegram of the 13th of March, 1913, Monsieur Iswolski gave Monsieur Sazonow an account of a conversation he had had with Noubar Pasha in Paris. The latter had declared "that the Armenians placed all their hopes in the powerful protection of Russia and were ready to follow the advice of the Russian Government in all circumstances." Boghos Noubar had elaborated a plan of reform for which he begged the support of Russia. Iswolski asked him to take no steps without the consent of the latter.†

In March and April an avalanche of telegrams was sent from the Russian consuls at Bitlis, Erzerum and Van, announcing the preparations for massacres. Giers telegraphed that the Armenians were much alarmed by events in Bitlis, Erzindjian, Hadjine, etc., and that he was afraid of a conflagration in

* Telegram from Vorontzoff-Dachkoff of the 7th of February, 1913. (Document No. 12.)

† The Tiflis Records, Document No. 14.

Asia Minor between Musulmans and Christians.* These telegrams served as a prelude for the Russian Government's negotiations with the Cabinets of Europe in order to obtain an international mandate for the pacification of the six vilayets. The date for the massacres to be announced was carefully chosen. On the 22nd of May and the 5th of June, Sazonow informed his Ambassador in Berlin that he had just given orders to Giers "to elaborate in conjunction with his English and French colleagues the principles to serve as a basis for the attitude of the Triple Entente regarding the Armenian question." He suggested that the plan of 1895 might serve as this basis. Finally, on the 24th of May (7th of June new style) in a circular telegram, Neratoff, the Russian Under Secretary of State for Foreign Affairs, formally placed the question of reforms before the Cabinets of Europe.†

This circular of the 7th of June quickly obtained the support of France, and, with more difficulty, that of England and the other Powers. The Armenian question was officially opened. As early as the 9th of June, a Commission consisting of the three Ambassadors of the Triple Entente was formed in Constantinople to elaborate a plan of reform to be submitted to the other Ambassadors. On the 10th of June, Germany and Austria-Hungary consented

* The Tiflis Records, Documents Nos. 17, 18, 19, 21, 24, 28.
† *Ibid.*, Documents Nos. 31, 32.

to discuss the problem, though demanding that the integrity of Turkey should be safeguarded. On the same day Sazonow ordered Giers to take the initiative with the Grand Vizier, as far as Russia was concerned, and to tell him that " it now depended on Turkey to unite herself by close ties with Russia."* Meanwhile Germany had raised difficulties. Jagow, although instructing Wagenheim, the German Ambassador in Constantinople, to take part in the deliberations, expressed doubts as to their utility and declared that a conference of Ambassadors could not have the weight of a supreme tribunal. Moreover, Berlin and Vienna both insisted that a representative of Turkey should take part in the deliberations, a demand which Giers and Sazonow regarded as inacceptable on the pretext that the presence of a representative of the Porte would upset the preliminary elaboration of the plan.†

This plan was elaborated by Monsieur André Mandelstam, the first dragoman at the Russian Embassy, and was based on the plan and the *Note* of 1895, drawn up by the three Ambassadors of France, England and Russia, the *irade* of the Sultan of the 20th of October, 1895, the plan for a legal code drawn up by the European Commission of 1880, and the Statute of Lebanon. Mandelstam's plan, which was adopted by the Triple Entente, provided the

* The Tiflis Records, Document No. 39.
† *Ibid.*, Documents Nos. 40, 41, 43.

basis for the deliberations of the Powers. Its fundamental principle was the formation of a single Armenian province, under a European Governor-General, independent of the Sublime Porte, to consist of the six vilayets of Erzerum, Van, Bitlis, Diarbekir, Kharpout, and Sivas, with the exception of certain frontier regions. The Ambassadors in Constantinople met together to discuss it. Giers was anxious to exclude the examination of the plan of reform elaborated by the Porte, but Germany and Austria-Hungary insisted that it should be taken into consideration.

The Porte had just communicated to the Powers the general outline of the reforms which it wished to adopt, reforms which according to Giers were " completely different " from the Mandelstam plan. The latter succeeded in preventing the preliminary discussion of the Turkish scheme by the Commission of Ambassadors who assembled on the 8th of July, 1913, at Yenikeuy, by opposing the proposal made by the Triple Entente regarding it.

The representative of Germany on the Commission opposed the idea of a single province of Armenia, pointing out that it would be too large and that the lack of means of communication would render the task of a single administration exceedingly difficult. Mandelstam, in the name of Russia, emphasized the necessity for Armenia to have " a strong and united will," and quoted the example of Crete, Lebanon, and Roumelia. The representative of Austria-Hungary observed that the nomination of a Governor who would be independent of the Porte was a slight on the sovereignty of the Sultan. Germany considered the example of Lebanon was not to the point, as Armenia was twenty-four times as large as Lebanon, and to have a similar administrative system for her as for the latter was equivalent to wishing to administer France on the pattern of Tarascon, and the Mandelstam plan looked like an attempt to separate Armenia completely from the Ottoman Empire. The creator of the Russian scheme nevertheless insisted upon the necessity for a Governor-General who would be independent of the Porte. Supported by Fitzmaurice, the English representative, Monsieur Mandelstam tried with true legal subtlety to prove that a State can remain a sovereign State even if it submits to foreign control, provided it does so with its own consent. The task which lay before Europe was precisely that of persuading Turkey to consent to foreign control; that once secured, her sovereignty would be safeguarded. He was anxious for a decision that the Porte should not longer have the right of transporting soldiers from other districts into Armenia, nor of settling *mouhadjirs* there, in order that Turkey might be completely disarmed against the machinations of Russia.

It is obvious from the demands made by Monsieur

André Mandelstam in the name of Russia, how determined was the latter to humiliate Turkey. Talaat endeavoured to settle the question directly with the Armenian members of the Turkish Chamber; but without success. The Armenians refused to separate themselves from Russia, although Talaat offered to increase the number of Armenian seats in Parliament from fifteen to twenty.*

A few weeks after the failure of the Commission of Yenikeuy, on the 19th of August, 1913, Sazonow reopened the discussion of the problem with the Cabinets of Europe. He informed Berlin that the matter might become "acute," to which Zimmermann replied that to begin a partition of Turkey would be exceedingly dangerous.† Finally, after long drawn-out negotiations, Jagow instructed the German Ambassador in Constantinople to make concessions. Whereupon a fresh exchange of views between the German and Russian dragomans took place. At all events, a German Note on the Armenian question, dated the 10th of September, 1913, declared that "the German Government regarded it as neither possible nor advisable to force Turkey to submit to a decision which she did not accept willingly." Germany wished the Commission to resume its labours on the basis of the Turkish plan. At last, on the 23rd of September, Giers and Wangenheim came to

* The Tiflis Records, Document No. 62.
† *Ibid.*, Document No. 63.

an agreement regarding the disputed point as to how the two Inspectors-General were to be chosen, after having previously accepted the basis of two administrative sections instead of a single province of Armenia.* The six points of this Russo-German agreement settled the way in which the Inspectors-General were to be chosen *at the request of the Porte*, who was to appoint them for a certain term of office and give them full power over the officials and judges. For the electoral assembly of the two new sections the Russo-German agreement laid down the principle of equality in number between Musulmans and Christians, as well as equality in the holding of offices. The delicate point was the question of European control, and the formula chosen was that Turkey should *propose* that the Powers should undertake to superintend the carrying-out of the reforms through the instrumentality of their Ambassadors in Constantinople.

In a Note dated 26th October, 1913, Turkey replied to the six points of the Russo-German agreement, by saying that she was willing to carry out the reforms with the help of European advisers, but that she insisted upon preserving the integrity of the State. In the case of Giers, the Grand Vizier quoted the example of the English adviser, who, until the War, managed the Turkish Customs quite independently, although he was nominally under the

* The Tiflis Records, Document No. 78.

authority of the Turkish Inspector of Customs. The Porte refused to allow Europe to share in the *nomination* of the Inspectors-General, but she agreed to the appointment of European advisers for a period of ten years, on condition that she should have the right of applying for their appointment not to all the Great Powers, but only to one of them. She was ready to apply to Russia for two advisers for the two Armenian sections; but Giers regarded this as insufficient.*

Turkey increased her efforts to make Russia more accommodating. On one occasion Talaat offered Giers to choose 7,000 soldiers from the best Thracian regiments, in order to form them into a police force for the two Armenian sections to protect the Armenians against the Kurds. Giers replied that Russia would continue to claim her *right* to deal with the Armenian question by virtue of the Treaty of Berlin.† An attempt was made to bring pressure to bear upon Turkey by refusing to increase the Customs duty of 4%. England supported Russia in her request to Germany to insist upon the acceptance of the six points by the Porte. Finally the Grand Vizier accepted the necessity of applying for advisers to all the Great Powers, and of obtaining the previous consent of these advisers to every step taken, as well as allowing a delay of a month for the settlement

* The Tiflis Records, Document No. 91.

† *Ibid.*, Document No. 92.

of disagreements between the Inspectors-General and the advisers. But still Sazonow continued to make demands that the Porte regarded as inadmissible. After several weeks of interminable discussions, the Grand Vizier declared himself ready to apply semi-officially and by word of mouth to the Ambassadors for the appointment of candidates for the posts of Inspectors-General, and to communicate semi-officially the function of these Inspectors, after a preliminary agreement had been reached, the appointment to be for a period of ten years.

At last, on the 13th of January, 1914, Giers telegraphed to Sazonow to be content with the results obtained, because "the Great Powers would not support us if we were to make large demands." These results were concerned only with the fundamental principles. Discussions were still continued on the subject of the composition of the general councils. Turkey proposed proportional representation for the Councils of Diarbekir, Kharpout, and Sivas, and this proposal was accepted by Russia, though she still tried to have the settlement of *mouhadjirs* in the Armenian vilayets forbidden, after having vainly endeavoured to secure the principle of electoral equality in those districts where the Armenians were in an obvious minority. On the 7th of February Sazonow authorized the signature of the agreement, which was initialled and signed on the following day. Two months later, Turkey appointed the Dutchman Westenenk and the Norwegian Hoff Inspectors-General of the two new sections, choosing them from a list of five candidates presented by Russia.*

On the 16th of April, 1914, His Beatitude the Patriarch and Catholicos of all the Armenians, Kervork V., thanked Sazonow for the Russo-Turkish Convention, of which he was officially informed by Count Hilarion Ivanovitch Vorontzoff-Dachkoff, Viceroy of the Caucasus. In his letter the Catholicos wrote in dithyrambic terms of the devotion of the Armenian people and their "sympathy" for Great Russia and "her adorable sovereign," the King-Emperor, Nicholas II., whose will had once more summoned the Armenians upon "the stage of history."†

VI

It is no part of a study of the origins of the Armenian problem to pass judgment on events that are too recent and too complicated to admit of being decided according to the principles of equity. So I will make no attempt to adjudicate the responsibility for the pitiable condition of the Armenians owing to the World War. I will content myself with describing

* The Tiflis Records, Documents Nos. 116, 134, 156–7.
† *Ibid.*, Document No. 158.

as briefly as possible the two contradictory theories concerning it.

The theory of the Armenian revolutionaries is well known. On the analogy of the fable of the wolf and the lamb, they represent themselves to Europe as a race persecuted by a "criminal" Government filled with ferocious sentiments against Christians who are subjected to its authority by an "accident" of history; furthermore that this Government profited by the War in order to rid itself of them by exterminating them in hundreds of thousands. In a lecture given by Monseigneur Touchet, a French Bishop, before *L'Œuvre d'Orient* in Paris, in February, 1916, the number of Armenian victims was estimated at 500,000. It is impossible to check the figures, although they seem grossly exaggerated. What is certain is that a terrible tragedy was enacted on the Russo-Turkish frontier in the spring of 1915, when the Armenians were placed between the cross-fire of a life-and-death struggle. But the historical conditions in which this struggle took place and which I have examined at close quarters, would lead me to conclude that the fable of the wolf and the lamb deserves no consideration before an impartial tribunal.

According to the opposite view, held by observers who are not prejudiced against Islam,* it was the Armenian revolutionaries themselves who took the

* See the *Gazette de Lausanne* of 25th March, 1916.

initiative in the drama, by first of all massacring innocent Musulmans at Koms, in February, 1915, at the time of the first Armenian rebellion. The district of Mousche was the scene of the bloody preliminaries to this formidable Turco-Armenian duel, and if an impartial inquiry were made here, it might shed some light on the question, if indeed light can ever be shed on a country where so much hatred burns. The events of this tragedy are as yet but little known, for the pamphlets published by the Armenian revolutionary committees in Europe must be regarded with caution.* In April the Armenian revolutionaries seized the town of Van, established an Armenian "General Staff" there under the command of Aram and Vardan, which delivered up the town to the Russian troops on the 6th of May, after having "freed" the district of Van from Mohammedans. According to a Russian newspaper in Rostow, the number of Armenian volunteers who placed themselves under the Russian flag amounted to about four divisions, a whole army corps. "A provisional Government of Vaspourkan" (the Armenian name for Van) had already been established under Aram Manoukian, the Governor-General of the "first province of Armenia." This was divided on paper into fourteen large and small provinces awaiting

* The following are some of the titles: *Documents sur le Sort des Arméniens en 1915; La Défense Héroïque de Van; Les Massacres et la Lutte de Mousche Sassoun en 1915*. (Published at Geneva.)

the auspicious formation of a "Great Armenia" by the Tsar.

Amongst the most notorious of the Armenian chiefs was Karakin Pastemadjian, a former member of the Turkish Parliament, known by the name of "Garo," who put himself at the head of the Armenian volunteers at the time of the opening of hostilities between Turkey and Russia, and the Turks accuse him of having set fire to all the Musulman villages he found on his way and of massacring their inhabitants. It is known that the attempts made by Turkey to win the support of the "Dachnakzoutioun" party against Russia at the beginning of the War were repulsed in the month of September, 1914, by the Armenian Congress at Erzerum, which declared itself "neutral." Nevertheless the thousands of Russian bombs and muskets which were found in the hands of its members prove what this neutrality meant. And indeed the Turks attribute the Russian invasion of the north of Asia Minor to the behaviour of the Armenian bands whose attitude made the defence of the country exceedingly difficult.

The fact that the Kurds did not remain inactive in the face of this upheaval is certain. And that they constitute a devilish and pitiless force when provoked, is likewise open to no doubt whatever. The Armenians must have known to what they were exposing themselves in going over to the side of Russia. The explosion of the forces of hatred, the flame of which had been fanned for generations by the incompatible nature of these races, and exploited without mercy by Russia, was bound to occur whenever a matter of life-and-death brought them into conflict. No government in the world would have been able to prevent this hideous clash, especially under the conditions in which Turkey was placed from the social and political point of view. European diplomacy could not foment racial and religious troubles in this Empire for a century with impunity. It was obvious —and Albert Sorel, the great historian, prophesied it over thirty years ago—that the policy of partition must lead to a catastrophe in which the whole world would founder.

As for the attitude of Turkey, this can be explained by the psychological situation in which she was placed by Europe. The animosity of the attempt to blot her out of the map of the world, the adamantine pitilessness with which Russia planned her complete destruction, and the religious prejudices of which one of the most calumniated races in the world is the victim, goaded this country into one last struggle. When the terrible danger that threatened her from Russia became clear owing to the attitude of the Armenians, she did what every nation in the world would do in a moment of distress—she drove out of the theatre of war all uncertain elements. It is obvious that in a country so poor in means of transport and without any modern technical appliances, such a measure must be accompanied by terrible suffering, and that the innocent had to pay for the mad dream of an Armenia under the protection of the Tsar.

And it was Tsarism that was the great criminal that never ceased to bring trouble into the world of Islam ever since there have been Tsars, just as it tormented the Russian people themselves upon whom an evil fate had inflicted it. For the East the overthrow of the Tsars by the Russian people was the greatest event that has taken place for the last three hundred years. And what has happened in Asia since the Russian revolution provides a significant warning for any who would attempt to imitate the methods of the Tsars in Oriental politics. It is clear that the system of enslaving Asia beneath the heel of an egoistic Europe has had its day.